Socialisms

D0929016

Socialism has been characterized by the great plurality of movements that have existed under that name. This diversity still exists today and is carefully examined by Tony Wright in this new edition of his critically acclaimed work that now features a foreword by Tony Blair.

Tony Wright provides the reader with an invaluable guide for the various forms of socialism by examining the background and history that have provided the materials for different socialist traditions. He also asks a number of questions such as: Is socialism rooted in moral values or scientific doctrine? Who are its actors and agents? What are its methods? Is it statist or pluralist? This book demonstrates that the answers to such questions often blur the conventional dividing lines of socialist movements and ideologies.

This book will be essential for all students who need to make sense of the many different sorts of socialism. With a new chapter at the end of the book Tony Wright shows us how socialism also has a future by applying traditional values in new ways.

Tony Wright is MP for Cannock and Burntwood. Before joining the House of Commons in 1992 he was Reader in British Politics at the University of Birmingham.

Socialisms

Old and new

Tony Wright

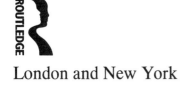

London and New York

First published 1996
by Routledge
11 New Fetter Lane, London EC4P 4EE

Simultaneously published in the USA and Canada
by Routledge
29 West 35th Street, New York, NY 10001

© 1996 Tony Wright

Typeset in Times by
Ponting–Green Publishing Services, Chesham, Buckinghamshire

Printed and bound in Great Britain by
Clays Ltd, St Ives PLC

British Library Cataloguing in Publication Data
A catalogue record for this book is available from the
British Library.

Library of Congress Cataloging in Publication Data
Wright, Anthony,
  Socialisms: old and new / Tony Wright. – 2nd ed.
     p.   cm.
  Includes bibliographical references and index.
  ISBN 0–415–15179–1 (alk. paper). – ISBN 0–415–15180–5 (pbk:
  alk. paper)
  1. Socialism. 2. Communism. I. Title.
  HX73.W75   1996
  335–dc20   96-26287
                                        CIP

ISBN 0–415–15179–1 (hbk)
ISBN 0–415–15180–5 (pbk)

For Jo, who had a heart, for ever

Joseph Philip Morys Wright
13 December 1982–22 August 1985

Nos da, cariad

Contents

Preface by the Right Hon. Tony Blair MP   ix
Preface to the second edition   xi
Preface to the first edition (1986)   xiii

1   Traditions   1

2   Arguments   18

3   Doctrines   35

4   Methods   52

5   Structures   69

6   Actors   87

7   Futures   105

8   A new socialism?   124

Further reading   150
Index   154

Preface by Rt Hon. Tony Blair MP, Leader of the Labour Party

For a number of years during the 1970s and 1980s, the Left was on the intellectual defensive. Across the western world, the Right dominated the battle of ideas. Having colonized the high ground of economic debate, it proceeded to apply a flawed belief in narrow individualism and crude market forces to whole swathes of society. It was spurred on by the fact that in Eastern Europe and the Soviet Union, centralized planning and the rule of one party disintegrated under the pressure of economic change and popular revolt.

A period of history came to a close with the collapse of communism in 1989. But a new era has opened up. It is marked by a degree of energy and activity on the left and centre-left not seen for a generation. It encompasses a range of interests and ideas. Its source is a rejection of the remedies of both the Old Left and New Right. And it speaks to a popular desire, clear and strong in Britain but evident elsewhere too, to move beyond some of the sterile debates of 1980s politics, and forge instead a new and radical agenda for the new century.

For the Left, that agenda will be dominated by the challenge of applying old values to new and radically changed circumstances. The collective must be mobilized to extend the freedom of the individual, the power of the private sector used to help serve the public interest, market and state joined in partnership not locked in conflict.

Tony Wright's book is an important route-map for this political journey. The book makes the simple but telling point that it is not and never was satisfactory to define socialism by state ownership and centralized planning. Ten or twenty years ago, this was not an argument that many people wanted to hear. Today it embodies the new common sense. It is the core values of democratic socialism that explain its power and durability as a political credo. And it is the reassertion of those core values that has been the heart of Labour's reconstruction over the last ten years. Social justice, community, responsibility and democracy are enduring themes in this book, and they are now firmly located at the heart of the Labour Party's new constitution. The revision of Clause IV mattered precisely because it concerned what it means to be a socialist at the end of the twentieth century. The truth brought out in this book is that the creation of 'new Labour' has taken the party back to its ethical roots.

The challenge now is to link these values both to a clear analysis of the condition of Britain today and to a compelling prescription for change. The debate is already moving on about how to build a stakeholder economy, how to make Britain one nation again, how to reform our politics to put power in the hands of the people and how to make Britain a leader in the new Europe.

Politics without ideas is barren. And ideas without values are weak. Far from an end of ideology, the end of the twentieth century is marked by its rebirth. This book is an important contribution to a critical battle of ideas and values that will shape our country for many years to come.

Preface to the second edition

It was only when someone pointed it out to me that I realized what this book was about. Once explained, it was clear that I had tried to think and write my way through the ferocious controversies on the Left in the 1980s in search of some secure theoretical and political ground. Disguised as a scholarly essay, it was really a contemporary argument. Its friendly reception suggested that others were engaged in a similar search.

The opportunity to bring out a new edition has enabled me to bring it up to date. Although it was written only a decade ago, the world with which it deals has altered dramatically. The great punctuation marks of the modern world now include 1989 alongside 1789 and 1917. Some of the intense arguments on the Left of just a few years ago already have an antiquarian quality to them. In Britain, social democracy has been engaged in a remarkable process of renewal.

The revised text reflects this new environment, adding to it and subtracting from it where appropriate, although I have deliberately not disturbed the essentials of the original and (mostly) resisted the temptation to rewrite history. However, I have added a new chapter in which I both review recent developments in Britain and extend the general argument of the book into the present.

This new edition would not have been possible without the enthusiastic encouragement of Caroline Wintersgill at Routledge, not for the first time, for which I am very grateful. Lucy Bailey came to change the world but agreed to change the text; and I offer apologetic thanks. Finally, I am especially grateful for a preface from the person who has done more than most to make it possible to write a new chapter.

Preface to the first edition (1986)

The title of this short book is neither a misspelling nor an originality. In setting out to write an introductory essay on socialism that would be accessible to both student and general reader, an approach was needed that could come to terms with the sheer variety of socialism. This variety is organizational and theoretical, historical and contemporary. It has been recognized in one way or another by almost everyone who has engaged with socialism, whether as friend, critic, or observer. However, the response to this recognition has differed.

Some socialists recognize it when they assert the credentials of their particular version of socialism and the illegitimacy of other versions. Some anti-socialists recognize it when they insist on an essentialist description of a nightmare socialism ('the end of all' in Lord Rosebery's phrase) in order to divert attention from the need for a more discriminating approach. It is also recognized by those academic writers on socialism who juggle with definitions and boundary markers in an effort to impose some order on their disorderly material. Others just give up in the face of all this, like the voice heard to exclaim at a Labour Party meeting, 'we don't want practical policies, we want socialist policies!'

In their different ways, all these approaches tend to regard the diversity of socialism as a problem. By contrast, the approach adopted here accepts this diversity as an essential part of what socialism is and has been, and as an important clue to its understanding. This does not mean that it is not possible to draw the boundaries of the socialist 'tradition' so wide that all particular traditions become in some sense part of the same family despite their manifest differences, but what sort of family is it that has, say, both Joseph Stalin and George Orwell among its members? Indeed, surely Orwell's own point in his telling satires, usually misread as attacks on socialism *tout court*, was that there were different *kinds* of socialism and that one (democratic) kind should be embraced and another (authoritarian) kind attacked.

So it is not perversity that prefers to deal less with a singular 'socialism' and more with a plurality of 'socialisms'. The aim is not to classify and label distinct traditions, nor to adopt ready-made labels, but to explore some of the terrain that has provided the materials for different socialist traditions. The chapters that follow focus on aspects of this terrain. First, the diversity of socialist traditions is sketched, along with the variety of socialist arguments. Then four key questions are identified and discussed, relating to the status of the socialist argument (moral value or empirical doctrine?), the means whereby socialist ends are to be achieved (reform or revolution?), the structural form of socialism (statist or associational?), and the leading socialist actors (classes or parties?).

These questions are set within the history of socialist ideas and movements, but they clearly remain as relevant as ever. Finally, against this background, contemporary socialisms are examined and some thoughts on their futures ventured.

Socialism has become an umbrella word, which its friends seek to shelter under (each trying to grab the handle or stab each other with the point) while its enemies wave it around indiscriminately hoping to beat as many opponents on the head as possible. There is no escape from this situation in the search for a 'true' socialism against which particular ideas and movements can be measured and judged. '*Moi, je ne suis pas marxiste*' was Marx's famous comment on some of his French followers, while R. H. Tawney remarked on the 'radiant ambiguities' of the word socialism. Such disagreements and tensions are regarded here as the subject matter of socialism, the basis of divergent traditions. These should be frankly acknowledged, not treated as marginal to an overarching unity.

Three further points follow from this. First, it will become clear that the dimensions of disagreement discussed here do not always neatly convert into the familiar demarcation lines between socialist traditions (for example, reformist social democracy versus revolutionary communism). Instead, other lines of affiliation and disaffiliation emerge. For example, there are reformist authoritarians (the Webbs, it will be recalled, fell in love with the Soviet Union), just as there are revolutionary libertarians (Rosa Luxemburg). Second, to acknowledge a plurality of socialisms is not to embrace the sort of sloppy pluralism that avoids the need for discrimination and judgement. By contrast, by rejecting the notion of a socialism that is historically or theoretically 'correct' it introduces the need for discrimination between kinds of socialism that may be more or less desirable, appropriate or plausible.

Third, this approach points attention to the extent to which one socialist tradition (namely 'Marxism') set its face against such socialist pluralism and endeavoured to secure for itself a position of organizational and theoretical monopoly. The argument here is that this project was illegitimate, its basis flawed, its consequences damaging, and that its disintegration is therefore to be regarded as both necessary and welcome. By extension, this suggests that one part of the contemporary socialist project involves a process of unlearning, and that at least some of what has now to be learnt is to be found in submerged, neglected and minority socialist traditions.

One final consideration is also relevant. This is the need for an approach that can accommodate not merely the evident historical diversity of socialist movements and ideas, but the actual status of socialism in the late-twentieth-century world. It is a world in which one person in three lives under a regime that describes itself as socialist, a fact which bears eloquent testimony to the success of socialism as a modern ideology, perhaps even *the* modern ideology. It is, however, also a world in which socialism has become 'socialism' whenever and wherever socialist regimes have come to power. In our time socialism ceased to be Left and became East. The old cry of 'socialism or barbarism' has become the new reality of socialism *and* barbarism. There is no 'socialist' society on which socialists would agree in bestowing the label. These uncomfortable facts must be faced, not least by those socialists who want to reassert a socialism of emancipation. The first fact, as G. D. H. Cole announced it a generation ago, is that 'socialism is no longer a single movement, making in a single direction'.

ACKNOWLEDGEMENTS

All writing runs up debts and, even if they cannot be repaid, they should at least be acknowledged. I want to mention three in particular, starting with the most general and finishing with the most special.

First, there is the indebtedness of a book like this to the work of all those authors whose scholarship provides the materials out of which its structure and argument are constructed. The fact that it has not generally been possible here to acknowledge such obvious debts individually makes it more necessary that they should be acknowledged collectively. The second debt is owed to the members of my evening class at the Birmingham and Midland Institute, who spent a lively winter discussing this book with me and in the process contributed a good deal to it. Not for the first time has an adult education class helped to make a book, and for an extramural teacher it is always the most enjoyable debt to be able to record.

Finally, though, by far the greatest influence on me during the writing of this book was the short, magnificent life of the person to whom it is dedicated. He changed everything and everyone he touched. It is really his book.

1 Traditions

> The resulting controversy, between many groups and tendencies all calling themselves *socialist*, has been long, intricate and bitter.
>
> (Raymond Williams)

The history of socialism is the history of socialisms. Moreover, it is a history not of fraternal plurality, but of rivalry and antagonism. The battle lines have often changed (Marxists versus anarchists, collectivists versus syndicalists, reformers versus revolutionaries, communists versus social democrats, Trotskyists versus everybody else, new socialists versus old socialists), but battle lines there have always been. Many socialists have reserved their sharpest arrows for attacks on other socialists, while almost all socialists have found it necessary to fight on at least two fronts at the same time. The arena of battle has also changed significantly over time, to take in new places, contestants, and traditions. The dramatic collapse of the communist regimes at the end of the 1980s is the most recent, and most momentous, development in this unfolding story.

WORDS AND TRADITIONS

The scene was set when Marx and Engels launched their first attacks on those early-nineteenth-century socialists they branded 'utopian' (in particular, Saint-Simon, Fourier and Owen). These writers, with their 'fanatical and superstitious belief in the miraculous effects of their social science', were judged to be not merely irrelevant to the developing class struggle but objectively reactionary in relation to it. In the same period Marx denounced the 'amateurism' of the 'French tendencies' (i.e. Proudhon) and set out to wage war on all such 'idealism' in the name of a scientific class theory. In the mid-1840s, solicited as a correspondent by Marx, the anarchist socialist Proudhon replied in these terms:

> Let us seek together, if you wish, the laws of society, the manner in which

these laws are realised, the process by which we shall succeed in discovering them; but, for God's sake, after having demolished all the *a priori* dogmatisms, do not let us in our turn dream of indoctrinating the people; do not let us fall into the contradiction of your compatriot Martin Luther, who, having overthrown Catholic theology, at once set about, with excommunication and anathema, the foundation of a Protestant theology. For the last three centuries Germany has been mainly occupied in undoing Luther's shoddy work; do not let us leave humanity with a similar mess to clear up as a result of our efforts. I applaud with all my heart your thought of bringing all opinions to light; let us carry on a good and loyal polemic; let us give the world an example of learned and far-sighted tolerance, but let us not, merely because we are at the head of a movement, make ourselves the leaders of a new intolerance, let us not pose as the apostles of a new religion, even if it be the religion of logic, the religion of reason.

This approach did not commend itself to Marx, nor to the Marxist tradition in general (a fact of some significance in view of the centrality of Marxism in the development of socialism). Socialism was not seen as a mansion with many rooms, but as a house of theory and practice in which dissenting traditions were shown the door in just that spirit of 'excommunication and anathema', of which Proudhon warned.

Marx emphatically and precisely saw the assault on, and defeat of, other available socialist traditions as an essential part of his original project (and a continuing preoccupation); so much so that he began by rejecting even the word 'socialism' because of its prevailing utopian connotations. The word had first appeared in England in the 1820s in an Owenite context, then in French usage in the 1830s. Its origins indicate its resonance. It was used to characterize the schemes of social reconstruction being advanced in England and France at that time by Owen, Saint-Simon and others, and to describe the adherents of these schemes ('socialists'). In seeking to counter such idealism, Marx needed a political vocabulary that would differentiate his position and distance it from these prevailing socialisms. Hence, in 1848, the world was presented not with the socialist but the *Communist Manifesto*. At this time the word 'communist' was associated with a more abrasive tradition, revolutionary, egalitarian and proletarian, as exemplified by Babeuf and the left wing of the French Revolution.

It was this tradition, of revolutionary class action, that Marx wanted to draw upon in opposition to the prevailing varieties of 'socialism'. Looking back forty years later, Engels wrote that 'We could not have called it a *Socialist* manifesto. In 1847, Socialism was a middle-class movement, Communism a working-class movement. Socialism was, on the continent at least, respectable; Communism was the very opposite.' Even in subsequent years, when usage had changed and blurred, it seems that Marx always retained a certain antipathy to 'socialism' as both word and concept (reflected in its pejorative appearances in *Capital*, usually referring to Proudhon and the utopians). However, as the nineteenth century progressed, socialism established itself as the general word and Marxism increasingly established its proprietorship over it.

Having entered this linguistic minefield, some further cautious exploration is appropriate. The diversity of socialist traditions has been reflected in the variety of socialist usage, and in the shifts in usage over time. Even when the linguistic ascendancy of 'socialism' was established, wrested by the Marxists from the utopians and the anarchists, 'communism' retained a variety of usages both old and new. For example, it was preferred by William Morris because it carried a traditional meaning of revolutionary class action to secure property in common. In England, at least, this served to distinguish it from Fabian 'socialism' in the 1880s and 1890s. The word could also refer to an original or primitive communism before class society, while it developed a further and more familiar meaning as a future, higher stage of social development beyond the socialism that would be the immediate successor to class society. It was launched on a new lease of life when, in 1918, the Bolsheviks appropriated it to mark their split from an allegedly degenerate European socialism and to claim an authentic historical pedigree. From that moment communism became Communism, and it was difficult thereafter to retrieve its other usages.

Matters were made no clearer by the fact that in becoming communists the Bolsheviks and their satellite parties did not relinquish their claim to be 'socialists' but instead now claimed to be the only authentic socialists. They sought to wrest any title to the name from the European socialist tradition that had called itself Social Democratic in the late nineteenth and early twentieth centuries as it combined its Marxist doctrine with party organization. In Europe before 1914 'social democracy' meant organized Marxism; after 1917 it came to mean organized reformism. The communists, appropriating Marx, not only denied the socialist credentials of social democracy, but attacked it (at one period as 'social fascism') as essentially reactionary and counter-revolutionary. Some socialists responded to these developments by coining the term 'democratic socialism' to describe a position that was non-communist and critical of undemocratic socialism as practised by the Bolsheviks, but at the same time was not merely reformist or ameliorative but remained committed to the reorganization of society on a socialist basis. This was a difficult position to sustain, but the need for it was a reflection of the fragmentation of socialism that had taken place. In a sense, democratic socialists were social democrats who meant it. A further linguistic footnote was provided by those social democrats in Britain who, in the early 1980s, became Social Democrats. Intended to signify their affiliations with a wider tradition, this change was also interpreted as an attempt to convert social democracy from a tradition *within* European socialism to a position outside and in opposition to it. It ended badly.

This excursion into the political language of socialism has raised many issues that will require further consideration later. For the moment, though, it is sufficient to record that the variety of socialisms is amply reflected in the varieties of socialist usage. This also serves as a reminder of those developments that have contributed to the evolution of socialism. For example, Marx's early antipathy towards 'socialism' is a reminder that there was socialism before Marx (just as there have remained socialisms alongside and outside Marxism). There is now socialism after Marx. The point here is not to play the familiar game of ransacking history for the precursors of socialism, from Thomas More to Plato and beyond, but to register the fact that the historical development of socialism has usually been viewed through the prism of the theoretical supremacy of Marx and the organizational dominance of Marxism.

This is especially the case with the 'utopian' socialists, traditionally dismissed by the Marxist tradition for their inferiority to the 'scientific socialism' that was developed by Marx and Engels. Indeed, the terms of this dismissal are such that it seems that the historical *function* of the utopians is to be superseded by Marxism. Yet the work of these early-nineteenth-century writers retains interest and significance, and does contribute to later socialist traditions. This is true of Owen's vision of social harmony through cooperation, of Fourier's scheme for community production that would nourish individuality rather than repress it, of Saint-Simon's plan for the reorganization of the social and economic order, and of Proudhon's mutualism that represented a form of decentralized producer democracy. When all the usual criticisms are made (that Saint-Simon did not mention capitalism, that Fourier was dotty, that Proudhon was full of contradictions, etc.), and when the obvious theoretical inferiority of these writers to Marx is acknowledged (as it loudly was by Marx), the fact remains that they did represent the first intellectual challenge to industrial capitalism and its ideology of liberal individualism, and did build a bridge to later socialist traditions.

Thus Proudhon nourished an anti-collectivist tradition, Owen a co-operative tradition, Fourier a libertarian tradition, and Saint-Simon a technocratic tradition. This indicates how misleading it is simply to dub them 'utopian', thereby suggesting a uniformity instead of the imaginative diversity of these early-nineteenth century socialisms. For Marx, however, they were essentially the same: not, as is usually suggested, because they could not say who was to bring about social change nor how they were to do it, but because they fundamentally misunderstood the nature of the social process. The lack of an agency was a reflection of this, as was their proclivity to indulge in moral appeals and undertake experiments in communal living. By contrast, Marx offered an account of the social process in which theory and practice were united and morality merged with necessity. Historical development was to be explained in terms of material forces which gave rise to forms of class society. Its present form was capitalism, or bourgeois society, a system of exploitation that operated through the extraction of surplus value from wage labourers. However, in creating a proletariat, capitalism had also created the agency whereby it would itself be transcended. The revolutionary victory of this exploited class, a particular class that was also a 'universal' class because it was the carrier of a general liberation, would mark the end of class society and the rediscovery by humanity of its essential (but previously estranged) species-being. Against such a prospectus, the offerings of the 'utopian' socialists could indeed seem rather paltry.

If there were socialist traditions before Marxism (or the foundations for such traditions), there were also socialisms alongside Marxism during the nineteenth century. Again, the tendency has been to view these traditions from the perspective of a Marxism that had consolidated its hold on European socialism by the final quarter of the century. Thus the progress of Marxism is conventionally charted in terms of Marx's intellectual victories over Lassalle, or political victories over Bakunin. Yet this obscures the extent to which a socialist tradition of state action in the conditions of a widening franchise (for example, associated with Louis Blanc in France and with Lassalle in Germany) was taking shape from the middle of the nineteenth century, and was not suddenly born in a later 'revisionism'. Similarly, Marx's contest with the anarchist Bakunin in the First International has often been presented by orthodox Marxists as an irritating distraction from the historic march of 'scientific socialism', instead of as evidence of the continuing appeal of a non-collectivist tradition that had been associated with Proudhon ('the master of us all' according to Bakunin) and which was to be taken up by anarchist communists like Kropotkin and by the syndicalists. There was also an insurrectionary tradition, linked with the name of Blanqui, that saw revolution not as the movement of a class but as the work of a conspiratorial elite of professional revolutionaries. Lenin was to provide a reminder of this tradition.

It is against this complex background that the period of ascendancy of Marxism within European socialism should be seen. This ascendancy was secured when, from the 1870s, socialism became both theory and movement with the development of workers' organizations in the main European countries. Because of its theoretical sweep, and the role it assigned to working-class political action, Marxism was well placed to provide the ideological underpinning of workers' parties. This was precisely the role that it did play during the period of the Second International from the late 1880s through to 1914. In the words of George Lichtheim, distinguished historian of socialism, Marxism 'functioned as an integrative ideology' in these years. However, it would be misleading to regard this apparent integration as evidence that the variety of socialist traditions had at last been reduced to unitary form. The attempt was certainly made to make Marxism perform this function; but the attempt failed.

The need for an integrative ideology was apparent to any observer of European socialism in the 1880s. Three main traditions were in evidence. There was Marxism, now organized as 'social democracy'. There was anarchism, and its anarcho-syndicalist derivatives. There was also reformism, most explicitly seen in English Fabianism but evident too in the democratic collectivism espoused by the 'possibilists' in France, headed by Paul Brousse. Thus the Second International was born out of two rival congresses convened simultaneously in Paris in 1889, by the Marxists and the possibilists (the latter were even alleged to have waylaid provincial delegates at the railway station and misdirected them to their own congress). The anarchists, meanwhile, devoted their considerable energies to causing disturbances at both of these congresses. The engine of the Second International was the German Social Democratic Party, which had itself been formed at a unity congress between the German socialists in 1875 at Gotha and had later adopted a thoroughgoing Marxist programme at Erfurt in 1891. This German party, led by Bebel and Liebknecht, then set about making the Second International in its own image.

It should be noted that socialism's centre of gravity, originally located in France and Britain, had now shifted decisively eastwards, to Germany. The Germans had created a united party and, in the face of the anti-socialist laws, had constructed an impressive organization and a mass following. By 1890 the party had won the support of about a fifth of the German electorate. Its prestige was enhanced by the traditional association of its leaders with Marx (until his death in 1883) and Engels (who lived on until 1895). It is not surprising that socialists elsewhere endeavoured to emulate the Germans by setting up their own Social Democratic parties, or that the Germans were the driving force of the Second International. They led the struggle against the anarchists ('anarchism' had now become the catch-all category to describe all disbelievers in a disciplined party equipped with a 'scientific' doctrine), and anarchist ideas were finally purged from the International in 1896. The Germans also endeavoured through the International to impose some unity on socialism in France, where the rich variety of socialist traditions was still much in evidence. The French Marxists, led by Guesde and organized since 1879 in the *Parti Ouvrier Français*, found themselves opposed on two socialist fronts by the syndicalists and the possibilists (as well as other independent groupings on the Left). These differences within French socialism kept spilling over into the International, an embarrassing reminder of socialist disunity.

Just as the German Marxists had dispatched the anarchists, they finally managed to discipline the wayward French socialists. At the 1904 congress of the International, in many ways its high-water mark, the 'revisionists' (notably Bernstein), who wanted to adjust both the economic and political analysis of Marxism in the light of changing circumstances, were roundly condemned and traditional doctrine reaffirmed. This position was then imposed on the member parties of the International and the French socialists were called upon to unite on this basis. This they did when Jaurès, socialist idealist and outstanding leader of French socialism until his assassination in 1914, agreed to bring his members into the new party, the name of which *(Section Française de l'Internationale Ouvrière*, SFIO) was a reminder of its origins. Thus French socialism was formally united from outside, an expression of the dominant position of German social democracy within European socialism and of its ability to impose an organizational model and doctrinal basis on the international movement. In turn, this enabled the International to engage in impressive displays of solidarity against bourgeois nationalism and war and in affirmations of international proletarian brotherhood. European socialism seemed to have forged a unity out of its divergent traditions, courtesy of the German social democrats. Moreover, this unity seemed to be rooted in a secure theoretical position.

This security was provided by 'Marxism'. The inverted commas are necessary here to indicate the role played by this body of doctrine during the Second International period. It should be recalled that the term 'Marxist' (and its variants) was originally deployed as a form of sectarian abuse against Marx's party, by Bakunin and his followers, a reply in kind to the language of sectarian vilification ('Proudhonism', 'Bakuninist', etc.) that Marx himself had developed and deployed. Gradually, however, the term lost its negative sectarian connotations and assumed a more positive orientation. The publication of the first volume of *Capital* in 1867 extended Marx's authority within European socialism, as did his role in the production of the basic documents of the International Working Men's Association (First International). The dramatic, if brief, revolutionary events of the Paris Commune in 1871 also had the effect of promoting Marx's reputation outside socialist circles. Thus, in the period between the First and Second Internationals the ideas of Marx and Engels became recognized as the basis of 'scientific socialism', of which they were the acknowledged founders. Their work now provided the reference point for socialist argument within and between different traditions, just as it also reshaped the conceptual vocabulary of socialism.

MARXISM AS IDEOLOGY

This extending influence in turn provided the basis for the mobilization of 'Marxism' as an integrative ideology by the Marxist element of German social democracy. It was not enough that the ideas of Marx should gradually be assimilated by the various schools of European socialism; Marxism-as-system should be established as the unitary doctrine of the international socialist movement. So 'Marxism' was marshalled into this role of official doctrine, an assertion of theoretical supremacy described (by the historian Georges Haupt) as 'this process of hegemonization'. This entailed an emphasis on its scientific status and completeness. The leading figure in this assertion of the ideological hegemony of Marxism was Karl Kautsky, theoretician-in-chief of German social democracy and dubbed the 'pope of Marxism', who deployed it against what he described as the prevailing 'eclectic socialism' (composed of elements from Marx, Lassalle, Bakunin, Proudhon, Rodbertus, etc.). The theoretical victory of Marxism would eradicate such eclecticism, and would also ensure the political victory of the Marxists. This process was encouraged by Engels, and the 'dialectical' materialism developed in his polemic against the materialist philosopher Dühring (*Anti-Dühring*) contributed greatly to the promotion of Marxism as a system. As a system, it was a self-contained proletarian science, and as such gave an intellectual backing to the social democratic political stance of separateness from the institutions of bourgeois society.

It was in this context that 'Marxism' functioned as the ideological underpinning of the Second International. It was deliberately employed in this way by the German Marxists, initially within German social democracy and then internationally. It was used to turn socialism into a unitary tradition, securely anchored in a body of scientific doctrine bequeathed by its undisputed founding fathers. Other traditions could be attacked in its name and their adherents brought to heel. Bridges could be built to it from more distant traditions, such as that elaborately constructed by Plekhanov from Russian populism. It was all very impressive. It was also a sham. Dissenting traditions were not in reality subsumed or subjugated, either by Marxist science or by political muscle.

This was evident in the resurgence of syndicalism that unsettled the ranks of social democracy in the late nineteenth and early twentieth centuries. Even in England, Beatrice Webb could note in her diary in 1912 that:

Syndicalism has taken the place of the old-fashioned Marxism. The angry youth, with bad complexion, frowning brow and weedy figure is nowadays a Syndicalist; the glib young workman whose tongue runs away with him today mouths the phrases of French Syndicalism, instead of those of German Social Democracy.

Similarly, despite the denunciation of 'revisionism' and the assertion of Marxist orthodoxy by the Second International, reformist tendencies had not in fact been suppressed either theoretically or practically. The revisionists had shattered the notion of a single, uncontestable, 'Marxism' at the level of theory, while the political practice of the orthodox was opening up a widening gulf between revolutionary theory and the actual business of social democratic politics. The period of the Second International has been called the golden age of Marxism. It was also the period when what Marx merely described as his theory of 'critical materialist socialism' was converted into 'Marxism' and presented as the complete theory of a unitary socialism. In fact, there remained other theories and a plurality of socialisms; and what seemed like an extension of Marx's ideas into a system really involved their contraction. Much of this was to become painfully clear in 1914 and subsequently.

TRADITIONS AND DIVISIONS

However, even in the years before 1914 it was already apparent that the Second International did not encompass all available socialisms, and that it was perfectly possible to be a socialist without also being a Marxist. It is true that in Europe as a whole most socialists were now Marxists, but this did not prevent many of them from interpreting the term in ways consistent with other traditions. In Britain, however, socialist traditions had developed since the 1880s that were non-Marxist and therefore quite distinct from the perspective of European socialism as a whole. The revival of socialism in Britain in the early 1880s, after the long interlude following the collapse of Chartism, certainly took the form initially of an attempt (led by Hyndman) to establish a Social Democratic party on the German model with a Marxist basis. The maturity of industrial capitalism in Britain, its large and increasingly organized working class, and the long residence here of Marx and Engels might be thought to have augured well for this attempt. Yet it failed, largely because of the developing force of other domestic traditions. Thus William Morris sought to integrate Marxist ideas with a Ruskinian tradition of aesthetic protest against the 'civilization' of commercial capitalism. Other anti-capitalist (though non-socialist) literary and cultural traditions were drawn upon in the development of an ethical socialism, involving a moral critique of capitalism and the presentation of socialism as a project for the remoralization of society. An ethical socialism of this kind, which came to be associated in particular with the Independent Labour Party founded in 1893, and was expressed by its leading figures, such as Keir Hardie and Robert Blatchford, became a dominant element in the ideology of British socialism. It was non-Marxist without also being anti-Marxist, in the sense that it was willing to acknowledge the importance of 'scientific' socialism even though holding that the essential socialist case was a moral one (and this did involve a rejection of the class theory of Marxism).

Ethical socialism was reformist, in terms of means though not of ends. However, the main school of British reformist socialism was Fabianism, the product of a small group of thinkers and writers (amongst whom Sidney Webb and Bernard Shaw were pre-eminent) who had founded the Fabian Society in 1884 and equipped it with a doctrine of gradualist collectivism, a doctrine that made its first major public appearance in 1889, in the famous collection of *Fabian Essays*. Fabianism was constructed out of an assortment of intellectual ingredients, notably from the nineteenth-century doctrines of positivism and utilitarianism, and out of the politics of advanced radicalism. It was not merely non-Marxist but anti-Marxist, in the sense that it challenged the basis of Marx's economic analysis and claimed to have developed a superior account of the nature of capitalist exploitation, and in the further sense that it rejected Marxism's strategy of revolutionary class action as wholly inappropriate to English conditions. Fabianism offered a strategy of 'resolute constitutionalism' (Shaw's phrase) that would increasingly capture the state, both centrally and locally, for collectivist purposes. This strategy was buttressed by a historical analysis that showed this process to be already well underway and the forces of individualism on the run. So here was a reformist tradition that stood at odds with the mainstream of European socialism before 1914, although it seems to have exercised some influence on the development of Bernstein's revisionism during his period of London exile. According to Rosa Luxemburg, Bernstein (whose *Evolutionary Socialism* became a classic text of socialist reformism) 'constructed his theory upon relationships obtaining in England. He sees the world through English spectacles.'

English exceptionalism was to be ended in 1914, but so was much else besides. The collapse of the Second International was the end of an illusion, or rather several. When the German, French, and Austrian socialists responded to the patriotic call in 1914 and voted for war credits, this not only killed the International but also the illusion of international proletarian solidarity. It shattered the illusion of social democracy as an independent force outside the institutions of bourgeois states. It revealed the illusion of a unitary socialism, both internationally and theoretically. It exposed the gulf between Marxist theory and social democratic practice. Above all, perhaps, it not only ended an era in the history of socialism but inaugurated a new era in which all socialist traditions were to be profoundly transformed. In the words of James Joll, a historian of the Second International, 'the Socialist world was never to be the same again after 1914'. Kolakowski extends the point: 'The summer of 1914 saw the beginning of a process whose consequences are still with us, and whose final outcome cannot be foreseen.'

In socialist terms, the war began with the collapse of socialist internationalism and ended with the Bolshevik revolution in Russia. 'Overwhelmed by opportunism the Second International had died. Down with opportunism and long live the Third International!' Lenin's response to the events of 1914 marked the beginning of a formal rupture within socialism, a rupture that was to dominate its subsequent history for much of the rest of the twentieth century, until the whole communist pack of cards came crashing down in 1989. It was a rupture that Lenin deliberately engineered, as he insisted that what had been revealed was the degeneracy of the whole pre-1914 social democratic tradition. This had preached Marxism but practised reformism. This had claimed to stand apart from bourgeois society but had thrown in its lot with that society at the moment of test. Of course, Lenin was right about all of this, but this is less significant than the conclusions he drew from the indictment. One reasonable conclusion that might have suggested itself was the need to amend theory in the direction of practice, but this was not likely to commend itself to Lenin as he organized the Bolsheviks for revolution in Russia. Instead he sought to make Bolshevism the centre of a new, authentic, revolutionary tradition that would integrate Marxist theory and practice and provide a rallying point for all those socialist elements who rejected reformism and were committed to the international class struggle.

The victory of the Bolsheviks in Russia turned this from a doctrinal position into an organizational project. It was a project that was to split the ranks of socialists everywhere, and to compress the variety of socialist traditions into two antagonistic camps. The major socialist tradition, Marxism, was appropriated as the official ideology of a regime, an elevation sealing it off for more than a generation as a living source of socialist ideas. During the period of the Second International, Marxism had at least functioned as an open orthodoxy, with no coercive power over heretics, which had to sustain itself in argument conducted at an impressive theoretical level. It was now destined to function as a closed orthodoxy, with its official interpreters, who could sustain their interpretations through their command of the machinery of a totalitarian state. Some socialists in Europe, notably the Austro-Marxists, endeavoured to maintain a Marxist position that was independent of Leninism, but this remained a minority enterprise in a hostile political environment. Marxism had become Marxism-Leninism, with few prepared to quarrel about the hyphen.

Other departures in nomenclature identified the rupture within socialism that took place in the decade after 1914. After seizing power, Lenin's party signalled their repudiation of 'social democracy' by adopting the title of 'Communist' in 1918. In that year the Russian Social-Democratic Labour Party (Bolsheviks) renamed itself as the Communist Party of the Soviet Union (Bolsheviks). It was the assertion of a historical pedigree in Marxist terms and a distancing from the social democracy of the Second International. One of the celebrated Twenty-One Conditions governing admission of parties to the new Communist (Third) International, adopted in 1920, made this abundantly clear. Member parties would have to take the label 'Communist', and far from being a point of detail this was 'a political one of great importance'. In the words of the document:

> The Communist International has declared a decisive war against the entire bourgeois world and all the yellow, social democratic parties. Every rank-and-file worker must clearly understand the difference between the communist parties and the old official 'social democratic' or 'socialist' parties which have betrayed the cause of the working class.

It is almost impossible to exaggerate the significance of what happened between 1914 and 1924. In the period before 1914 the socialist world did, with some exceptions and dissenting voices, achieve at least the appearance of organizational and theoretical unity. During the decade after 1914 this was converted into organizational and doctrinal warfare between two rival camps. Communist parties were licensed in Moscow by the Third International to wage war on non-Communist socialist parties throughout the world. The reconstruction of a Socialist International in 1923 in response to this was an acknowledgement of the permanent nature of the split that had taken place. Socialism was polarized between communism and social democracy, each claiming a unique socialist legitimacy. However, if the pre-1914 attempt to create a unitary socialist tradition had broken down, the subsequent compression of socialist traditions into the two organized camps of official communism and official social democracy was perhaps no less inadequate. It left no room for an independent Left that was nourished by traditions unsympathetic both to a communism that was authoritarian and to a social democracy that, partly in response to the communist challenge, had moved further in the direction of mere reformism. The brief attempt in

1920 by an assorted group of non-aligned socialists to organize a socialist 'centre' between parliamentarism and Bolshevism (in the so-called 'Two-and-a-Half International') had failed. It was not really the case that there were just two socialist traditions, which could be organized into rival armies, but for a long time it did seem so. This was, incidentally but not unconnectedly, also the time when fascism was able to make its malevolent advance.

DISINTEGRATION – OR DIVERSITY?

This brief sketch clearly does not exhaust the significance of the developments it describes. There also took place a fundamental shift in what may be called the geography of socialism, with far-reaching implications. The socialist centre of gravity shifted eastwards during the nineteenth century, from Britain and France to Germany, and with the Bolshevik capture of power in Russia it moved still further east in the early twentieth century. However, this geographical movement also represented a dramatic break with many of the leading assumptions of pre-1914 socialism. These traditional assumptions were economic, social and cultural. Their combined implication was that socialism would succeed capitalism (the fact of succession was of course a further assumption) in those countries that had a mature capitalist economy with a developed class structure, and that socialism would inherit and extend the democratic machinery and cultural capital of such societies. The success of Bolshevism challenged all of these assumptions, which is why so much theoretical ingenuity was employed by the communists to accommodate what had happened in terms of Marxist doctrine and to integrate it into a general prospectus for world revolution that would encompass the heartlands of industrial capitalism. The collapse of that prospectus was to require still further ingenuity in doctrine in an increasingly convoluted attempt to keep up with the shifting demands of domestic and international policy.

However, the changed geography of socialism did not present problems merely for the communist tradition. The non-communist, social democratic, and democratic socialist traditions were now presented with a world in which socialism was no longer merely a theoretical and organizational project but the self-description of an actual regime (and, later, of a cluster of related regimes). Further, this was a regime which, apart from its replacement of private by public property, seemed not merely to lack but positively to outlaw the democratic rights and individual freedoms that had always been promised, indeed assumed, as an essential part of the socialist project. Thus, from 1917 until 1989, social democrats and democratic socialists have had to pursue their version of socialism in an environment in which 'actually existing socialism' has meant something else. This has had a profoundly damaging effect on socialist fortunes in Europe and beyond, and has provided invaluable ammunition for the opponents of socialism in the propaganda battle for electoral support. In this sense, as Isaac Deutscher once remarked, the Russian Revolution 'has acted as a deterrent to revolution in the West'.

A further shift in socialist geography also took place. If communism pulled the socialist centre of gravity eastwards, the contrary pull exercised by the social democratic tradition now located itself in western and northern Europe, notably in Britain and Scandinavia. Thus Britain, which stood outside the main current of European socialism during the period of the Second International before 1914, became from the 1920s a leading representative of the non-communist socialist tradition. Meanwhile, anarchist traditions survived in southern Europe, especially in Spain. Behind this geographical fracture there lurked a larger question, or rather a cluster of related questions. Perhaps the idea of a single socialism was not merely historically or theoretically flawed, but culturally inadequate. Instead of a universalist socialism, experience seemed to suggest that there could be different sorts of socialism just as there were different sorts of societies.

Russia seemed to show that there could be a socialism, defined in terms of strategy and form of rule, in societies without mature capitalist economies, large working classes, and developed political institutions. Equally, the social democratic strength in those countries of Western Europe which were stable capitalist democracies seemed to suggest that a socialism of another kind also required a particular cultural base. Of course, one response to such lines of thought has been to deny the legitimacy of some kinds of socialism. Thus the Soviet Union was said, by some socialists, to be not 'really' a socialist country; and social democratic parties are also said, by other socialists (or sometimes the same ones), to be not 'really' socialist at all. Another response to the same difficulty, on the part of some socialists, has been to accept the legitimacy of all parties and regimes describing themselves as socialist, despite their manifest differences, because, in a fundamental sense, all socialists are necessarily on the same side. Both of these responses, though very different, share a common attachment to a unitary view of socialism. In other words, while they differ on what socialism consists of, taking a sectarian or catholic view of the matter, they both agree that there is *something*, in the singular, that socialism is. To challenge this is not to relapse into the sort of disabling relativism that suspends all critical judgement, but it is to insist from the evidence that there are demonstrably different *kinds* of socialism, which seem broadly to correspond to different kinds of societies. This was evident, at the level of doctrine, before 1914; and received ample practical demonstration after 1917. It is likely to be no less true of the world after 1989.

The need to think in terms of a variety of socialisms reflecting different national and cultural environments was argued even before 1914 by the Austro-Marxist Otto Bauer. Of course, the national dimension of socialism was a matter of more than passing interest to a socialist in the multinational Austro-Hungarian empire, but Bauer's argument that 'the cultural character of each nation stamps itself on its socialism' had general application. One of its implications, as Bauer himself wanted to point out, was that different national traditions should be allowed to pursue their own kind of socialism in their own way. Intended originally as a contribution to the pre-1914 debates within Marxism on the 'national question', the point was to become of more pressing practical significance later. The new Soviet state soon revealed in the repressive treatment of its own nationalities what Lenin's theoretical discussion of national autonomy actually amounted to. Equally, the communist Third International (Comintern) rejected in both its doctrine and its practice any notion of there being a plurality of socialisms as it enforced its own Moscow model on the communist parties that it controlled. In the memorable phrase of Léon Blum, heir of Jaurès and leader of French socialism between the wars, the French Communist Party was '*un parti nationaliste étranger*'. The irony, of course, was that the Soviet Union was itself a monument to the impact of national traditions on the form that socialism had taken (or, as the Russian poet put it, 'Peter the Great was the first Bolshevik').

In the post-1945 world, considerations of this kind assumed new interest and importance. On the one hand, in Western Europe the social democratic parties moved further towards reformism and a permanent accommodation with liberal capitalism in response to what were perceived as the social and economic changes taking place in these societies. The clearest formal signal of this accommodation was the adoption of the revisionist Bad Godesberg programme by the German Social Democrats in 1959. In the same way, the adoption of a 'Eurocommunist' perspective by the leading communist parties in Western Europe, involving a new polycentrism in their relations with Moscow, also represented a form of accommodation with the 'national' traditions within which they operated (exactly what else it represented became clear only later). The events of 1968, that *annus mirabilis* of postwar radicalism in the West, meanwhile confronted the communist parties with their worst fears about being outflanked on the Left. More dramatically, outside Europe there had developed new socialist regimes and new socialist movements. Many of these, from Maoism to 'African socialism', explicitly wanted to emphasize the national and cultural particularity of their traditions. They clearly needed to do this, partly to fit the facts, but also because of the evident distance of their experience from some of the central assumptions of classical western socialism (in terms of economic development, class structure, nationalism, and much else besides). Not surprisingly, perhaps, those reared in classical Marxism often reacted dismissively to the 'Marxism' of Third World socialisms (thus Maoism was an 'infantile parody' of Leninism to Lichtheim, and 'childish' to Kolakowski). Though doubtless justified, their reaction further points to the need to think in terms of a plurality of 'socialisms' rather than a single model.

It should be said again that this emphatically does not mean an indiscriminating relativism. It does involve some relativism, in so far as it allows that some forms of socialism – just as some forms of conservatism – may be more appropriate to certain types of society (for example, that democratic socialism is tied in a significant way to the developed capitalist democracies, or that – in Baran's words – 'socialism in backward and underdeveloped countries has a powerful tendency to become a backward and underdeveloped socialism'). This does not avoid discrimination, though, since the fact that a certain kind of socialism may be more or less appropriate to a particular society does not thereby make it more or less desirable or worthy of support.

It was sometimes argued, not least by some western socialists, that the sort of socialism that was established in the Soviet Union was appropriate to the needs and character of that society. This argument, that communism in some sense 'worked' in a way that capitalism did not, did not look as implausible in the 1930s as it came to look later (a shift encapsulated in Khrushchev's remark about the effect of measuring Soviet output in terms of tons being that Russian chandeliers invariably brought ceilings crashing down). Yet even if an argument about appropriateness could have been sustained, this did not make Soviet communism any less tyrannical or more deserving of support from those who described themselves as democratic socialists. Perhaps this is clearer in the post-communist world at the end of the twentieth century than it was in an earlier period.

What the account here has sought to show is that the modern world has been full of socialisms of different kinds. There has been no unitary tradition. On one view, this represents a process of theoretical disintegration. On another and more feasible view, though, it is an indispensable reminder that socialism has always been distinguished by its diversity. During the long period, intensified by the Cold War, when this diversity was compressed into the two opposing blocs of official communism and a rival social democracy, it could easily be overlooked. It now reappears, along with the sort of traditions that sustained it. However, it reappears in a context where the communist tradition has collapsed but where social democracy is also called upon to renew itself in the face of the collapse of many of its own former assumptions. This is a context in which it becomes a matter of some importance to identify not merely the variety of socialist traditions but also the essential ideas upon which they are based. That is the purpose of what follows.

2   Arguments

Socialism, however, is obviously a word with more than one meaning.

(R. H. Tawney)

The diversity of socialist traditions has been reflected in the variety of socialist arguments. The familiar question 'what is socialism?' therefore requires a less familiar answer. If there is not a single socialist tradition but a plurality of traditions, then the ideas and arguments associated with these traditions have to be discussed in similarly plural terms. So the question should more properly be asked as 'what are the ideas and arguments of what kinds of socialisms?'

DEFINITIONS AND DIFFICULTIES

There is no shortage of available definitions of what socialism is, but there is a shortage of agreed definitions. Indeed, how could it be otherwise? Much harmless fun may be had in definition swapping, as long as there is no expectation that this will yield a form of words that encompasses the variety of the thing described. What is possible, of course, is to define the characteristics of a particular kind of socialism, existing or aspirational, preferred or disparaged, but this is a different enterprise (though often passed off as the same). Thus it may be possible to define 'democratic socialism' in terms of certain essential characteristics, although the adjective indicates an initial act of differentiation and the terms of the resulting definition are likely to leave many open spaces at the level of policy and practice (where it matters). Still, it is both possible and desirable that such limited and limiting definitions are essayed, in order to clarify what is being described, defended, or attacked, but on the understanding that what is being discussed is a particular kind of socialism and not the attempted appropriation of the whole range of socialist traditions. Consider the following definitions of socialism, quickly culled from a shelf of socialist literature old and new. It is tempting to include Lenin's 'soviet power plus electrification', and Herbert Morrison's 'what a Labour government does', as the authentic viewpoint of organizational socialism (a strange coupling, of Lenin and Morrison, even turns out on this view to be rather less strange than it seems), but the temptation should perhaps be resisted. The following remain, all attempting to define what socialism essentially consists of:

> The condition of common ownership and control of the means of production, or at least an important part of the means of production, exercised at least putatively on behalf of the whole people without respect for special privileges, and at least putatively in compliance with their decisions.
>
> (Charles Taylor)

> A society is to that extent socialist in which it provides the possibilities for a free creative development of every individual.
>
> (Gajo Petrović)

> Equal division of the national income among all the inhabitants of the country, and the maintenance of that equal division as the invariable social postulate, the very root of the Constitution.
>
> (Bernard Shaw)

> An institutional pattern in which the control over means of production and over production itself is vested with a central authority – or, as we may say, in which, as a matter of principle, the economic affairs of society belong to the public and not the private sphere.
>
> (Joseph Schumpeter)

> A social order in which there is the maximum feasible equality of access, for all human beings, to economic resources, to knowledge, and to political power, and the minimum possible domination exercised by any individual or social group over any others.
>
> (Tom Bottomore)

> A social order founded on more social and economic equality, higher social and economic security, and greater emphasis on community values than are produced by the spontaneous development of an industrial economy under the profit motive.
>
> (Richard Lowenthal)

> The dominance of social ownership in the economy, together with political and economic democracy.
>
> (Alec Nove)

The greatest possible degree of conscious human control over the personal, social and natural environment exercised democratically.

(Gavin Kitching)

Even this brief and random definitional excursion well illustrates the difficulties involved in the attempt to pin socialism down. None of the definitions here acknowledges that it refers to a particular version of socialism, yet some manifestly do, as is evident from their elaborate conditioning clauses. The frequent emphasis on democracy makes this clear, for what these authors want is to distinguish their 'democratic' socialism from both the theory and practice of undemocratic socialism. For much of the twentieth century, this was a necessary obligation. For, as George Lichtheim has put it, 'One can have democracy without socialism, and vice versa. Whether the two can be effectively combined is the prime question of our age.' This question should not be ducked by pretending that democratic socialism is by definition the only 'true' socialism when it obviously is not. The history of the twentieth century makes this abundantly clear.

A secure refuge from such problems might be thought to be found in the assertion that socialism is essentially about the public ownership of the means of production, whatever else it might also be about. In other words, that socialism is non-capitalism. Yet this too is clearly inadequate, certainly if offered as a root definition. Partly, this is because socialists have disagreed about both the importance and the extent of public ownership; but too, because a system of public ownership may well also be inegalitarian and undemocratic and therefore a denial of what many socialists would want to regard (*pace* Lichtheim) as basic socialist objectives. There is the further difficulty that public ownership may be centralist (as Schumpeter insists it has to be), although this is a conclusion that would be resisted by those socialist traditions that are decentralist and libertarian.

A more promising path would seem to be that offered by attempts to define basic socialist values (such as equality and fairness) and then to give effect to these values in terms of structures and procedures (such as public ownership and redistributive taxation). In other words, we should first define socialism by its values or goals, then explore the appropriate means whereby such ends might be realized or advanced. Yet this approach, despite its obvious merits, would be rejected by those socialists for whom values have no independent status outside particular modes of production and who hold that the establishment of a socialist mode of production is the precondition for the realization of socialist (i.e. universal, non-class) values. Socialists of this kind, as will be seen, tend to dismiss a socialist moralism that deals in the language of justice and equality as so much petit-bourgeois distraction. Even if this dismissal is disallowed, a socialism of values still faces formidable difficulties in achieving definitional coherence and a distinctive identity. For example, socialism may be about equality, but of what kind and how much? Moreover, if there is not a single socialist value but several, as seems likely (for example liberty and equality, individuality and community), what if there is tension between these several values and how are such tensions to be resolved?

In face of all this, it is scarcely surprising that a sample of socialist definitions of the kind assembled here ranges from the prosaic and institutional (public control of the means of production) to the most audacious and humanistic (free creative development of every individual). Of course, as the most audacious of all versions of socialism, Marxism closed this gap effortlessly through a materialist method whereby the change in the mode of production effected by the victory of the proletariat is also the realization of the humanistic prospectus of unalienated creativity. Yet this remains only one version of socialism, despite its philosophical sweep and the traditional tendency of its adherents to regard it as a comprehensive system that had, so to speak, all the answers. The questions remain, and other socialisms have contributed their own answers. Is socialism to be seen as the victory of a class or the triumph of an idea? Is it the fulfilment of a more general political and intellectual tradition or a rupture of that wider tradition? Is it a science or a morality? Is it revolutionary or evolutionary? Centralist or libertarian? These and other questions have long provided the material for different socialist traditions, and for a variety of socialist arguments.

COMMON AND UNCOMMON GROUND

In looking at some of these arguments, one can see that the earlier definitions suggest a possible starting-point. They indicate that socialists are interested in the promotion of certain social objectives (such as equality and community), and also that they have regarded the control of the means of production as of central importance as far as such objectives are concerned. The common starting-point for these positions, which has also been the point of departure and divergence, is the socialist critique of the social and economic order spawned by capitalism. This order is variously referred to as the market society, bourgeois society, liberalism, or individualism. Whatever the term used, it is intended to describe a society in which self-interest-pursuing, contracting, competing individuals stand as the basic units, traditional social ties are dissolved, the autonomy of economic life from ethical constraints is established, and there are no general social objectives apart from those deriving from the rational pursuit of self-interest. The authentic note of such individualism was famously expressed by Dickens in *Hard Times*:

It was a fundamental principle of the Gradgrind philosophy that every-thing was to be paid for. Nobody was ever on any account to give anybody anything, or render anybody help without purchase. Gratitude was to be abolished, and the virtues springing from it were not to be. Every inch of the existence of mankind, from birth to death, was to be a bargain across a counter. And if we didn't get to Heaven that way, it was not a politico-economical place, and we had no business there.

It is against such individualism that socialists have traditionally mounted their indictment. Indeed, 'socialism' as a view of human sociality is advanced in opposition to that of competitive individualism. The political economy of individualism is attacked for its production of wealth for the few and misery for the many. Thus the indictment of individualism carries with it the two basic socialist positions: the concern with certain values, and the claim that such values are negated because of the appropriation of the means of production by a class. So socialist arguments have been hammered out of the assault on capitalism and its philosophy of individualism. The contrast between the new socialism and the old individualism was set out interestingly by Sidney Webb in his *Socialism in England* (1890) in Table 1.

It is the assault on individualism, the ideology of 'free' capitalism, that has always been the common ground of socialist arguments. It represented the ideological veneer that concealed the real character of capitalist exploitation. Its competitive, self-regarding values thwarted human co-operation and fraternity. It stunted the individual personality and destroyed the possibility of real community. It elevated private greed and ignored public need. The terms of this indictment are common to the whole range of socialist literature, though the presentation may vary. It at least establishes socialism as what it is not, and what it is against. It is non-capitalism (at least in unconstrained form) and anti-individualism (not to be confused, of course, with anti-individuality). Yet this remains a negative identification, and conceals the extent to which from this common basis socialist arguments have taken different, and often conflicting, forms. Socialists may all be against capitalism in some sense, but not necessarily on the same grounds; and they may all be in favour of socialism, but again for different reasons and understanding it in different ways.

This may be so at a quite basic level. For example, it has clearly been the case that some socialists, in attacking capitalism, have really been attacking the modernization process itself; while others have been enthusiastic modernizers and have attacked capitalism because of its inefficiency in this respect. Thus, early socialists like Fourier could attack the new capitalist 'civilization' for its atomism and corruption of natural passions and seek to restore a more organic community, while others, like Saint-Simon, could be

Table 1 The contrast between the new socialism and the old individualism

INDIVIDUALIST RADICALISM 1840–1874	SOCIALIST RADICALISM 1889
'That the best government is that which governs least.'	'That the best government is that which can safely and successfully administer most.'
Corollary. – Wherever you can make a 'soft place' for a contractor, do so.	*Corollary.* – Wherever the collective organization of the community can dispense with a contractor or other 'entrepreneur' it should do so.
'That the utmost possible scope should be allowed to individual enterprise in industry.'	'That, wherever possible, industries of widespread public service should be organized and controlled for the public benefit.'
Corollary. – The best social use to which you can turn a profitable monopoly is to hand it over to some lucky individual to make a fortune out of it.	*Corollary.* – Every industry yielding more than a fair remuneration to the actual managers should be 'municipalized' or 'nationalized', or else specially taxed.
'That open competition and complete freedom from legal restrictions furnish the best guarantees of a healthy industrial community.'	'That only by gradually increasing legal restrictions can the worst competitors be prevented from ousting their better rivals.'
Corollary. – John Bright's opinion that adulteration is only a form of competition: the 'individualism' of Mr Auberon Herbert.	*Corollary.* – 'The answer of modern statesmanship is that unfettered individual competition is not a principle to which the regulation of industry may be entrusted.' (Mr John Morley, 'Life of Cobden', Vol. 1, ch. xiii, 298.)
'That the desired end of "equality of opportunity" can be ultimately reached by allowing to each person the complete ownership of any riches he may become possessed of.'	'That Political Economy indubitably proves "equality of opportunity" to be absolutely impossible of even approximate attainment, so long as complete private ownership exists in land and other economic monopolies.'
Corollary. – The policy of the 'Liberty and Property Defence League'.	*Corollary.* – The policy of 'Nationalization' or 'Municpalization' of land and other economic monopolies.
'That the best possible social state will result from each individual pursuing his own interest in the way he thinks best.'	'That social health is something apart from and above the interest of individuals, and must be consciously pursued as an end in itself.'
Corollary. – 'Private vices, public benefits'.	*Corollary.* – The study of the science of sociology, and of the art of politics.

Source: Sidney Webb, *Socialism in England*, 1890

excited by the prospect of the new 'industrialism' and seek to realize its potential by releasing it from its individualist constraints. In attacking capitalism, socialists have looked both backwards and forwards, to a lost past and to a new future. This suggests a wider ambiguity within socialism in relation to the age it confronted. On the one hand, socialism was the creature of the Enlightenment, an expression of the spirit of the age. On the other hand, it stood against the age, and carried a Romantic protest against the new society. This ambiguity is evident with Marx, whose early (and continuing) conception of unalienated, 'whole' man stands alongside a conception of a ruthless process of modernization at the hands of a capitalism destined to create the conditions for socialism. The fact that socialism was seen as the condition for creative, unalienated man may be thought to resolve this ambiguity, or it may be thought instead merely to make it stand out in sharp relief. What is certainly the case is that much of the early argument between Marx, Proudhon and Bakunin was grounded in their different orientations to the age they confronted, and their arguments have continued to give different directions to socialist thought. Nor should it be thought that such questions have been resolved: socialists continue to resist the 'logic' of modernity on one side, while on another side they have emerged as its leading agents, in unexpected places.

This problem of the status and orientation of socialism has always been particularly apparent in its relations with liberalism. Was liberalism to be rejected as the ideological creature of capitalism (as the indictment of 'individualism' suggested), or was the liberal tradition of the Enlightenment to be incorporated into and fulfilled by socialism? Behind this question there lay another: did socialism mark a rupture from existing society, or its further development? Socialism's negative consensus, its assault on capitalist individualism, could too easily serve to prevent any direct engagement with these questions. It was enough to expose the ideological character of liberalism and the classbound nature of its general claims. When socialists used the language of 'wage-slavery' they intended to confront liberalism with the hollowness of its most celebrated emancipatory achievement. Yet this did not resolve the ambiguity surrounding socialism's own relationship to the dominant liberal tradition. On one view socialism stood apart from the entire edifice of bourgeois society, in its own separate and self-contained proletarian culture, equipped with its own proletarian science, a preparation for the time when the bourgeois order would be overthrown and the new society established. Instead of continuity, there was comprehensive opposition, and comprehensive rupture and final transcendence.

On another view, however, the task of socialism was to extend and fulfil the prospectus of liberalism, by converting its claims from class into universal terms. If the former view provided the basis for revolutionary communism, the latter became central to the modern social democratic tradition. This tradition acknowledged that it was part of the same cultural universe as liberalism, and in challenging liberalism claimed to be extending it in ways that fulfilled its emancipatory mission. Thus it was claimed that liberty had to be nourished by equality if it was to be universalized, and that this involved extending its scope from the civil and political sphere into the social and economic. 'There is actually no really liberal conception that does not also belong to the elements of the ideas of socialism', wrote Bernstein; while Jaurès announced that 'only socialism will give the Declaration of the Rights of Man its entire meaning'. On this view a socialist was a liberal who really meant it, just as (in the words of a German socialist in 1868) 'democracy must become social democracy if it honestly wants to be democracy'.

ARGUMENTS AND AMBIGUITIES

The ambiguity about liberalism has been reflected in the range of socialist argument, and has had a considerable impact on socialist politics. This was particularly the case after 1917 as socialism shifted its centre of gravity from Western Europe, and therefore also away from the liberal inheritance itself. It could no longer be assumed that socialism would build upon the cultural foundations of liberalism, or that socialism would be essentially free and democratic. This had been the assumption of the Second International Marxists, but such essentialism could not be sustained after the Bolshevik revolution, when it became necessary either to repudiate the liberal tradition or to affirm socialism's connection with it. The experience of fascism made matters even more pressing, as socialists had to confront the question of whether to make common cause with 'bourgeois' democracy in the face of something demonstrably worse. What these experiences did reveal was the range of tensions within the general socialist position during the twentieth century, tensions that served to sustain divergent socialist traditions.

To put this in another way, it is clear that the socialist argument has historically been put in a variety of terms, and that at least some of these represent quite different kinds of socialism. For example, a libertarian socialism has always confronted an organizational socialism. The former has depicted the release of individuality consequent upon the eradication of the oppressive structures of class and state, and has often thought in terms of the self-direction of small communities. It deploys the language of freedom and spontaneity to describe its purpose. By contrast, organizational socialism focuses less upon the unfreedom of capitalism than upon its disorder. It seeks to replace the chaos of capitalist competition, wasteful and undirected as it is believed to be, with socialist planning and efficiency. The work of Saint-Simon provides the clearest early source for this type of socialism, with its insistence that the new industrial society required a new system of organization capable of rational planning. In particular, this involved the replacement of 'politics' by forms of 'administration' run by the key producer groups, 'so as to form a general system of organization directed towards a great common industrial goal'.

Yet here was an advocacy of planning as scientific rationality that was not also statist and centralist. Indeed, it explicitly rejected political centralism in favour of forms of producer self-management as the appropriate organizational model (thereby enabling Durkheim to make his celebrated appropriation of Saint-Simon for his own version of worker socialism, and more generally to attach anarchism to socialism through the connecting thread of producer democracy). In general, though, organizational socialism has embraced the state and central planning as its instruments, and has resisted those socialist currents advocating decentralization and producer control. This has been as true of such reformist traditions as Fabianism, with its collectivism that sought 'to gather the whole people into the State' as Shaw put it, as it has been true of the communist regimes that ruled in Eastern Europe. This is why the advocates of a libertarian, self-managing socialism have for so long had to operate outside the definitions of socialism offered by both the mainstream social democratic and the mainstream communist traditions.

Socialism as rationality has always sustained much socialist argument. Capitalism is here indicted less for its injustice and exploitation than for its sheer irrationality as a means of organizing economic life. Indeed, the injustices of capitalism, its production of wealth for the few and misery for the many, have been presented as a consequence of its inability to arrange economic and social life in a rational manner. Thus H. G. Wells (in his *New Worlds for Old*) described how the socialist

> wants a complete organisation for all those human affairs that are of collective importance. He says, to take instances almost haphazard, that our ways of manufacturing a great multitude of necessary things, of getting and distributing food, of conducting all sorts of business, of begetting and rearing children, of permitting diseases to engender and spread are chaotic and undisciplined, so badly done that here is enormous hardship, and there enormous waste, here excess and degeneration, and there privation and death. He declares that for these collective purposes, in the satisfaction of these universal needs, mankind presents the appearance and follows the methods of a mob when it ought to follow

the method of an army. In place of disorderly individual effort, each man doing what he pleases, the Socialist wants organised effort and a plan.

On this view, then, socialism was not the victory of an exploited class but the triumph of reason. Competition was wasteful and chaotic, and prevented society from solving its collective problems.

This has been a fundamental socialist argument. It places socialism squarely in the Enlightenment tradition and presents it as the most plausible contemporary carrier of this tradition. It further presents socialism not as the project of a class but as the general project of a rational humanity. This has given socialism an appeal for members of those groups (intellectuals, scientists, etc.) who are, as it were, professionally interested in this project. It also helps to explain, for example, the wide appeal of Soviet planning in the 1930s when compared with the consequences of capitalist competition and disorganization elsewhere. The fact that the Soviet Union 'had no unemployment' could easily, too easily, make it seem a beacon of socialist rationality in an irrational world, an example of what would be possible if capitalist competition was replaced by socialist planning. However, it also illustrated the tendency for socialist rationality to turn into an enforced rule of reason, whether by a Leninist party endowed with superior consciousness or by Beatrice Webb's 'elite of unassuming experts' (the fact that the Webbs fell in love with the Soviet Union should be seen less as personal idiosyncrasy and more as an example of the strange affinities generated by a socialism of social discipline and rational order). Socialist rationality required its guardians, just as it required the suppression of 'irrational' elements.

Of course, socialism may be seen as *both* a class project *and* the general project of a rational humanity. Instead of the establishment of a system of socialism-as-rationalism being regarded as the remedy for the ills suffered by an exploited class, the victory of that class could be seen as the remedy for the ills suffered by humanity as a whole. The belief that this was so could lead easily to the view that nothing was more important than the victory of this class, to which all else should be subordinated, since the future of humanity itself depended upon it. Most socialists have framed their arguments in terms of class categories, at least in the sense in which they have depicted capitalism as a system of class exploitation and socialism as the means whereby such exploitation would be ended or at least checked; but they have differed on the extent to which socialism is exclusively a matter of class analysis and class action. If socialism is about classes, is it not also about individuals? If it is about class power, is it not also about social justice? If it is about class exploitation, is it not also about other forms of exploitation? If it is the movement of a class, is it not also a general movement of people?

SCIENCE AND HISTORY

Such questions serve to mark out different socialist positions. Marxism has in the past provided the basis for one set of answers, with its emphasis on the centrality of the mode of production and its class character in giving society its decisive shape. Marx's celebrated formulation of this position in the 1859 Preface to *A Critique of Political Economy* provides a marker:

> In the social production of their life, men enter into definite relations that are indispensable and independent of their will, relations of production which correspond to a definite stage of development of their material productive forces. The sum total of these relations of production constitutes the economic structure of society, the real foundation, on which rises a legal and political superstructure and to which correspond definite forms of social consciousness. The mode of production of material life conditions the social, political, and intellectual life process in general. It is not the consciousness of men that determines their being, but, on the contrary, their social being that determines their consciousness.

The terms of this formulation have provided the material for much socialist argument over the years. The intense disputations and intricate exercises in textual exegesis associated with it may have something of an antique air now, but the argument remains central to any understanding of socialism's theoretical history.

Some of this argument has been of the 'what Marx really meant' kind, with much dancing on the terms 'condition' and 'determine' in a bid to hammer out the extent to which Marx was, or was not, a determinist and the purveyor of social laws. Certainly many Marxists have read him in this way, but that may not be altogether Marx's fault. Similarly, other socialists have rejected what they have taken to be Marx's determinism even when they have accepted his general account of the centrality of the mode of production. Traditionally, Marxists have adopted a more or less rigid attachment to the base-superstructure model of society as the universal tool of social analysis, whereas there have been other socialists who have wanted to assert a much more independent role for elements of the 'superstructure' (such as politics and the state) and to operate within this space for socialist purposes. What Marx's formulation does reveal, however, is the essentially class character of his analysis and the repudiation of other approaches, including those of other socialists. Marx's units are classes not individuals, for individuals have social significance only in terms of class membership and they are in every sense socially determined beings. For Marxism this raised questions about the generation of socialist consciousness and the process of social change, but for other socialists it represented an unacceptable devaluation of what it meant to be an individual human being.

This basic difference was reflected in other implications of Marx's production theory of society. It carried with it a rejection of any view of socialism that involved the framing of desired ends or values and then the construction of means towards their realization. Such an approach simply did not make sense in terms of a production theory of social determination. It was utopian, idealistic, unscientific. Similarly, Marx's productionism was at odds with those versions of socialist distributionism that sought to reallocate social goods in terms of such notions as 'equality' or 'justice', for this was an inherently individualist approach of claims and rewards that obscured the real determinant of social allocation, namely the class character of the mode of production. Thus, Karl Kautsky explained how an early socialism that had been preoccupied with principles of distribution had been superseded by a socialism that realized that 'the distribution of products in a community is determined ... by the prevailing system of production'. Some socialists, and most of the critics of socialism, might persist in treating socialism as a theory of distribution, but it was essentially a theory of production. This enabled Stalin to dismiss the idea of equality of consumption as 'a reactionary petty-bourgeois absurdity worthy of some primitive sect of ascetics'.

Such a dismissal carried all the weight of scientific socialism behind it. It serves as a reminder of the extent to which socialism for much of its history sought to present a scientific doctrinal face to the world – although this has not been its only face. Socialism as social morality has coexisted, not always easily, with socialism as social science. The Marxian distinction between socialism 'scientific' and socialism 'utopian' was designed to bury the latter, an act of historical burial that came to be widely accepted; notwithstanding the fact that a 'utopian' like Saint-Simon claimed to be essentially a social scientist while the 'scientific' Marx, at least on one view, looks like the supreme utopian. The scientific socialists have presented socialism as the science of society, able to explain the determinants of social structure and the motor of social change. They have seen socialism as *essentially* scientific, equipped with a historical science that identifies the determining role of the mode of production in historical change, a social science that identifies the class basis of contemporary society, and an economic science that identifies the process of capitalist exploitation. The scientific socialist has claimed to be in possession of a comprehensive and self-contained method of social analysis that has yielded a body of truths. Both the method and the truths were defended resolutely, because they constituted the distinctive status of socialism. It was left to other socialists to distinguish the scientifically true from the ethically desirable, and to give some attention to the latter.

The scientifically true also has a habit of becoming the historically inevitable. Much socialist argument in the past has been sustained by a comforting sense that history was on its side. This is as true of the reformist Fabians who pointed to the relentless, historical march of collectivism as it is of the revolutionary Marxists who confidently awaited that historical moment when capitalism would finally collapse and the proletariat would inaugurate socialism. In *Capital* Marx described the process that would usher in the great historical climax:

> Along with the constantly diminishing number of the magnates of capital, who usurp and monopolise all the advantages of this process of transformation, grows the mass of misery, oppression, slavery, degradation, exploitation; but with this too grows the revolt of the working class, a class ever increasing in numbers and disciplined, united, organised by the very mechanism of capitalist production itself. The monopoly of capital becomes a fetter upon the mode of production, which has sprung up and flourished along with it and under it. Centralisation of the means of production and socialisation of labour at last reach a point where they become incompatible with their capitalist integument. This integument is burst asunder. The knell of capitalist private property sounds. The expropriators are expropriated.

Here is a historical drama the script of which is already written, and with the proletariat required to act out its necessary role at the appropriate historical moment. It produces the old familiar picture of socialists waiting for capitalism's final and decisive crisis, when the proletariat will fulfil its historical task. It has turned out to be a long and fruitless wait.

Not all socialist argument has been of this kind, of course. Many socialists have denied that there is anything historically necessary about socialism, for there could be other successors to capitalism even if capitalism was to collapse. Similarly, the working class could well fail to act in the way scripted for it. Whether or not socialism was historically necessary, this by itself did not make it desirable. So some socialists rejected history in favour of action, whether the sort of insurrectionary action that cut across any nice judgement about historical ripeness or the balance of forces, or the gentler sort of action that involved the pursuit of a freely chosen ideal. When R. H. Tawney urged people to 'choose equality' it was an invitation to make history, not simply to respond to its alleged imperatives.

VALUES AND PLURALITY

Among socialists who have taken values seriously, there has been wide agreement that equality should be regarded as a key socialist value, perhaps even *the* socialist value. Socialism has addressed itself to the structure of society, and sought to replace the unequal social structure of market capitalism with a structure of equality. At bottom, this involves a moral commitment to equality as a value, for it would not be enough to expose existing inequalities without also mounting a case for equality itself (and in moral terms that withstand defences of inequality on the assorted grounds of liberty, enterprise, welfare, etc.). Thus socialists, from a variety of perspectives, have anchored their commitment to equality in a view of the equal worth of all individuals, and have presented their egalitarian proposals as extensions and applications of this basic position. Tawney's *Equality* remains perhaps the most powerful and sustained argument of this kind, but even this also serves as a reminder that there are difficulties in concluding that socialism is essentially about equality (as was argued, for example, by C. A. R. Crosland in his *The Future of Socialism*). Partly this is because socialists have disagreed about what is involved in a commitment to equality, stretching from the sort of militant egalitarianism that makes equality its single, absolute value ('Let there be no other difference between people than that of age or sex', in the words of Babeuf's *Manifesto of the Equals*), to the moderate egalitarianism that distinguishes equality of treatment from identity of treatment and addresses itself to the elimination of unjustifiable inequalities.

However, this is not the only difficulty involved in enthroning equality as socialism's sovereign value. There is the further difficulty that socialism espouses not one value but several, and socialist positions are forged out of this cluster of values. For example, socialists have embraced equality but they have also embraced liberty, unwilling to allow the latter to be appropriated by individualism. Some socialists have mistakenly invented a 'socialist' liberty that has nothing to do with its 'bourgeois' version (just as they have invented a socialist 'democracy' that has nothing to do with bourgeois parliamentarianism), but other socialists have wanted to be both equal and free and have advanced an argument for equality that is not only sensitive to the claims of liberty but seeks to extend and strengthen it. Indeed, in some socialist arguments equality is advanced *for* liberty, as the means whereby the positive freedoms of activity and choice are enlarged for most people. 'The aim of socialism', declared Clement Attlee, 'is to give greater freedom to the individual.' This is not the only sense in which equality begins to look like an instrumental socialist value, the servant of other values, in socialist arguments. What seems to be a case for equality as the central socialist value frequently turns out on closer inspection (as with Tawney) to be a case for the role of equality in promoting such values as fraternity, fellowship, citizenship and community; and it is these that are considered fundamental.

This suggests a further point about the nature and extent of socialism's ultimate claims. These have ranged from the prosaic to the transcendental. Socialism has stood for welfare and security, claiming to end the miseries of poverty and unemployment caused by capitalism. If it is objected that this is not 'socialism', the short answer is that many socialists have believed that this is precisely what socialism is about. Other socialists have gone beyond this welfare objective to suggest that in fulfilling objectives of this kind socialism has wider consequences for social life, producing, for example, a greater 'serenity', as Aneurin Bevan once described it, or a growth of cooperation, community, and fraternity. Yet this does not exhaust the range of socialism's claims. It has been possible to envisage, as with Owen, a transformation in human nature consequent upon a change in its social environment. Most ambitious of all, as with Marx, socialism has been presented as nothing less than a prospectus for rehumanization, the recovery of human unity and subjectivity consequent upon the abolition of socially determined human alienation. In this 'dream of perfect unity' as Kolakowski describes it, there is a fusion of political and civil society, of collective man and individual man, of social life and private life. It is one of the many ironies in socialism's history that such a fusion was indeed achieved in the twentieth century, and in the name of Marx, but scarcely in a form that Marx would have recognized as the emancipatory realm of self-determining creativity. Whether the dream has nourished the nightmare is another matter, with its own history.

What emerges from all this is that there is no single socialist argument, just as there has been no single socialist tradition. Moreover, there is not merely a plurality of socialist arguments, but tension, ambiguity, and even conflict between them. Table 2 attempts to indicate, in shorthand, some of the forms that the socialist argument has taken.

It should be emphasized that the list in Table 2 is intended simply to illustrate some of the terrain and tensions of socialist arguments. It is not exhaustive, and other terms could have been employed at almost every point. Nor are the couplings intended to denote opposites, for often it is a matter of emphasis or approach. Moreover, actual socialist positions can and do accommodate different approaches, for example doctrine *and* values, rationalism *and* moralism, equality *and* liberty. Yet the differences are important, not least because they have sustained different socialist traditions. Scientific, doctrinal socialism has taken its stand on different ground from ethical socialism. A socialism that is immanent in history is not the

Table 2 Forms of socialist argument

Doctrine	Values
History	Action
Determinism	Voluntarism
Revolution	Reform
Production	Distribution
Rationalism	Moralism
Centralism	Decentralism
Class	Individual
Equality	Liberty
State	Community
Modernization	Restoration
Welfare	Wholeness
Order	Self-management
Bureaucracy	Democracy

same as a socialism that attaches itself to human energy and will. A socialism that builds down from the state differs from one that builds up from the community. An organizational socialism of order, planning, and bureaucracy rubs up against a libertarian socialism of direct democracy and self-management. A reformist socialism of improvement and persuasion has a different basis from a revolutionary socialism of rupture and transcendence. A socialism that promises more security, more equality, more freedom, or simply more 'decency', to use Orwell's term, has different ambitions from a socialism that promises a total transformation of every aspect of human existence – and so on.

Such tensions do not themselves constitute distinct socialist traditions, but they do indicate the sort of terrain on which different kinds of socialism have developed. In practice, of course, socialist arguments take different forms in different places, as well as in the same place over time. New evidence and experience extend the range of argument or change its focus. Thus the experience of 'actually existing socialism' demanded a response from a doctrinal socialism that had maintained a particular position in relation to the determining character of the mode of production. Likewise, feminism raises questions for a socialism that has traditionally fixed its eyes on the exploitation of class in the waged economy but has had a blind spot for the exploitation of gender in the domestic economy. The changing character of the global economy, the late-twentieth-century resurgence of market liberalism, the shifting structures of class and the fracturing of traditional communities, all these and more test and develop the repertoire of socialist argument. As arguments develop and are restated, so socialist theories are reassessed (as in the endless reincarnation in the not so distant past of Marx as economic determinist or revolutionary humanist). Socialist positions are constructed out of real and inescapable tensions (for example, between state and community, planning and freedom, egalitarianism and diversity, solidarity and opportunity, regulation and markets), unless it is believed that no such tensions exist and that there is only one kind of socialism. At the end of the twentieth century this is a difficult belief to sustain. Moreover, the great Marxian 'synthesis' that once claimed to resolve all socialism's internal tensions has long since fallen apart under their strain, along with the regimes that claimed to have been constructed upon its basis; but so too has the post-1945 social democratic settlement in the West, which has come to be decisively unsettled.

Before considering where this leaves socialism, in any of its forms, it is necessary to inquire a little further into where it has come from and what may be learnt from this history of ideas. Most of what follows is therefore concerned with exploring the variety of socialism by looking more closely at what have traditionally been some of its central questions and tensions. Is its method that of reform or revolution? What is the structural form of socialism? Who are the actors who are to bring socialism about? However, an even more fundamental question requires some attention first.

3   Doctrines

> Put in the simplest and most basic terms, socialism has both an empirical theory and a moral doctrine.
>
> (Bernard Crick)

Beneath the variety of socialist arguments, about ends and means, strategies and actors, there lurks a more basic distinction affecting the form that these arguments have taken. Indeed, it is a distinction that defines the status of socialism, in the sense that it indicates the essential foundations upon which socialist arguments are constructed. The distinction was glimpsed in the tensions discussed earlier, between science and values, rationalism and moralism. Socialism has presented itself as two kinds of doctrine, a positive doctrine of analysis and explanation and a normative one of morality and values.

KINDS OF DOCTRINE

To identify this distinction, and to insist on its importance, is not to suggest that actual socialisms can be neatly distinguished in terms of their different kinds of doctrinal basis. In practice, socialists have tended to be both rationalists and moralists, combining theoretical analysis with moral valuation. The two lines of doctrinal argument have been mutually supportive, each calling in the aid of the other to extend the argument and strengthen the position. For example, early British socialism was founded upon *both* the theoretical account of exploitation provided by the so-called Ricardian socialists with their labour theory of value *and* the Owenite moral indictment of market capitalism. This dualism continued to sustain British socialism later, as a Fabian rationalism with its theory of economic 'rent', which extended an analysis of exploitation to include the capitalist as well as the landlord (designed to trump both liberalism and Marxism) and was embodied in its doctrine of collectivism, was combined with the sort of moral arguments mounted by the ethical socialists associated with the Independent Labour Party. Moreover, if socialist moralists have readily augmented their critique of capitalism and advocacy of socialism with the armoury supplied by a socialist rationalism, even the most severely rationalist of socialists have often revealed, when lightly scratched, a soft underbelly of moralism.

Indeed, the metaphor of soft underbelly is less appropriate than that of tough inner skin. This is clearly the case with Marx, for the reader of *Capital* soon discovers that the analysis of capitalist exploitation is a matter not merely of political economy but also of moral passion. More generally, Marx's values, most prominent in the early, 'humanist' Marx but remaining central to his mature position, shape the view of socialist man that in turn sustains the whole socialist project. They are robustly republican values, and point towards the recovery of human subjectivity beyond capitalism. As Kolakowski puts it: 'the notion that Marx regarded socialism as a system for depressing individuals into a Comtean universal being deprived of all subjectivity is one of the absurdest aberrations to which the study of his work has given rise.' Even the dry old Fabians, with their elaborate exercises in historical sociology designed to establish the pedigree of collectivism, turn out on closer inspection to be rationalists in search of the conditions for moral unity and consensus in society.

So rationalists are moralists, and moralists are rationalists, whether they look like it or admit to it. This merely testifies to the fact that socialism is a doctrine in both the senses identified here, and necessarily so. It is a philosophical account of the moral superiority of socialism to capitalism, but it is also a theoretical account of how societies are actually structured and the determinants of this structure. This necessary dualism may seem to devalue the significance of the distinction that forms its basis, yet this is not so when viewed against the historical development of socialism itself. In this light the distinction between the two kinds of doctrine takes on a considerable significance, not least because it has been regarded as significant by socialists themselves as they have sought to construct general socialist positions on the basis of it. Doctrine as theory has not always gone hand in hand with doctrine as values, even if they are necessary and natural partners and despite the fact that their coexistence may be detected where it is not normally expected or even where it is formally denied. Some socialists seem to have contented themselves with a sort of moralistic whistling in the wind, a comforting stance that could prove disabling (as Ramsay MacDonald, for example, discovered) when hands had to be dirtied in the engagement with capitalism and with office. Other socialists have repudiated the language of values altogether and wrapped themselves in a 'scientific' doctrine that has all the answers, a stance occasioning its own trail of disabilities and disasters in the face of a historical process that, perversely, has gone on asking new questions.

When Marx first opened fire on the utopians he described his target as 'doctrinaire socialism'. By this he meant systems of society that were the mental inventions of particular thinkers ('petty bourgeois'), utopian constructions that corresponded to the undeveloped state of the class struggle. He wrote the following in his *Poverty of Philosophy*:

> So long as the proletariat is not yet sufficiently developed to constitute itself as a class, these theoreticians are merely utopians who, to meet the wants of the oppressed classes, improvise systems and go in search of a regenerating science. But in the measure that history moves forward, and with it the struggle of the proletariat assumes clearer outlines, they no longer need to seek science in their minds; they have only to take note of what is happening before their eyes and become its mouthpiece . . . From this moment, science, which is a product of the historical movement, has associated with it, has ceased to be doctrinaire, and has become revolutionary.

So here is the original distinction between a doctrinaire (utopian) science and a revolutionary science, with the elevation of the latter and devaluation of the former. One is ultimately baseless (and becomes reactionary), while the other is securely rooted in the historical process itself and represents the viewpoint of the class that is the progressive agent in that process. Thus socialists such as Proudhon were to be denounced because they did not understand this process and simply invented unavailable and historically regressive social orders, while indulging in a merely moralistic criticism of the competitive system.

Here, then, is the repudiation of one version of 'doctrinaire' socialism and the development of another. The object of attack is a false and undeveloped conception of what constitutes a scientific approach, as well as the whole appeal to morals in socialist argument. It should be repeated that the 'utopian' socialists themselves made extravagant claims to scientific status, as evidenced by Saint-Simon's belief that he was the founder of the new science of industrial society. It should also be recalled that the nineteenth century was the period when the Enlightenment tradition prompted social thinkers of all persuasions, influenced by the prestige of the natural sciences, to set about constructing a science of society. The historical development of societies came to be widely regarded as a patterned process, and assorted attempts were made to translate these patterns into social laws that pointed forwards as well as backwards in their explanatory ambitions. These considerations are relevant to any understanding of the sense in which

Marx came to be regarded as the founder of 'scientific socialism' and thus of an entire tradition.

This is difficult and still contentious ground, but a number of points need to be made for present purposes. For example, it is necessary to register some distinction between Marx and the 'scientific' Marxism constructed out of his legacy. It seems fairly clear that he was not in the business of imitating the physical sciences, even though he was not unwilling to trade off some of the favourable associations to which such imitation gave rise. As already seen, his own 'science' claimed to be rooted in the observable reality of historical development and social movements, unlike the 'fantastic' science of the utopian socialists. It was essentially a claim to be engaged in empirical theory, in the sense in which Lichtheim could say that 'it was only after Marx had intervened that socialists began to understand how capitalism actually worked'. It was not a claim, therefore, to have discovered the 'iron laws of history', as was frequently alleged. Indeed, late in life Marx ridiculed the notion of 'using as one's master key a general historico-philosophical theory, the supreme virtue of which consists in being super-historical'. Instead, Marx's production theory of society was to be seen (as he said) as a 'guiding thread' that indicated general conditioning factors, not as laws of iron determination. Thus, modern interpreters of Marx's work are properly able to present his social theory as essentially a 'research hypothesis' (the phrase belongs to Terrell Carver, one such interpreter).

However, when all this is duly registered, something more still needs to be said. If Marx's general social theory, with its focus on the central role of technology and the mode of production, can be treated in this way, the same is not true of his narrower economic theory, with its account of value and surplus value and of the dynamics of capitalism's contradictions, crises, and collapse. In no sense does this have the character of a research hypothesis; it carries the certainty of verifiable causal analysis. Moreover, it is this Marx, the mature economist and scientific analyst of capitalism, who was to provide the basis for a subsequent, comprehensive 'scientific socialism' armed with economic laws. Furthermore, even if Marx's social theory is presented in terms of the identification of certain tendencies rather than as a system of rigid determination, the fact remains that it was regarded by its author as a system. It was all-embracing and self-sufficient; it did not require the further advance of knowledge in the social and human sciences or contributions from other disciplines; and while there might be other socialist doctrines there was only one that had scientific status and social significance.

So here was a doctrinaire socialism, partly in the necessary sense of open, empirical theory, but also in the closed sense attaching to a particular view of what constitutes a science. Two further features can be noted at this point. First, Marx's doctrine claimed to combine analysis and action, theory and practice, understanding the world and changing it. This involved, crucially, the identification of an agency through which such a combination would be effected, and through which the historical process would work itself out. For Marx, of course, this agency was the proletariat, but the discovery of this agency looks more like a philosophical act on Marx's part than an empirical one. In the formulation to be found in *The Holy Family*:

> It is not a question of what this or that proletarian, or even the whole proletariat, at the moment regards as its aim. It is a question of *what the proletariat is*, and what, in accordance with this *being*, it will historically be compelled to do. Its aim and historical action is visibly and irrevocably foreshadowed in its own life situation as well as in the whole organisation of bourgeois society today.

If Marx can be at least partially acquitted of some of the wilder charges of historicism and scientism of the kind levelled by many of his traditional critics, it nevertheless remains the case that his position represents more than a method, or set of analytical tools, as suggested by some contemporary Marxists. It extends into a doctrine about the direction and agency of historical development that encompasses the future as well as the past and culminates in a communism that is presented as nothing less than the end of 'prehistory'.

Second, in terms of the kinds of socialist doctrine identified here, Marx's position represents the most unequivocal and fundamental repudiation of socialism as moral doctrine. To repeat the point, this has nothing to do with the question of whether Marx himself was animated by values, a question to which an affirmative answer has already been given. What is central here is Marx's assertion that the indictment of capitalism had to be grounded in historical and economic analysis and not in any independent moral argument. Indeed, any such belief in an independent moral arena was fundamentally misconceived, since it failed to recognize the dependence of moral positions and even the terms of the moral vocabulary upon material interests.

Ethical considerations were therefore irrelevant to the analysis of capitalism, as irrelevant as the attribution of moral responsibility to individual capitalists or the belief that individuals enjoyed a social and moral significance apart from their class position. As Marx explained in the preface to *Capital*:

> Individuals are dealt with only in so far as they are the personification of economic categories, embodiments of particular class relations and class interests. My standpoint, from which the evolution of the economic formation of society is viewed as a process of natural history, can less

than any other make the individual responsible for relations whose creature he socially remains.

Further, it was equally misconceived to think in terms of the working class defining the values that would constitute their emancipation and then setting about the task of realizing them through action. There could be no separation of this kind, for it was only through the activity of emancipation in the historical process that the aims actually being pursued came to be understood. There could thus be no distinction between fact and value, between what is and what ought to be; nor between freedom and necessity. It is clear from this that not merely is Marx unable to provide socialism with an ethical basis or moral philosophy, but his formulation of the socialist project denies the need for any such provision to be undertaken.

FROM MARX TO MARXISM

These brief remarks are intended to get the character and status of Marx's doctrine into some sort of focus. This is necessary in order to navigate the crossing between Marx and Marxism in the latter part of the nineteenth century, a crucial period when Marxism not only consolidated its ascendancy over other versions of socialism, but also asserted its credentials as a comprehensive science of society. No longer was it to be presented, if it ever had been, as dealing in research hypotheses and methods of empirical enquiry, but rather as a rigid doctrine of economic laws and historical determination. Here was a fully fledged scientific socialism, a term proudly displayed and impressive in its range and scope. This consecration of Marx's work as scientific socialism was a development of considerable significance for the general history of socialism, as both movement and doctrine. It was a development that occurred first during the period of the Second International in the generation before 1914, then second and more durably when Marxism became the official ideology of the Soviet regime. Thus, in fact, two developments, both relevant to the discussion here, took place. The ascendancy of Marxism over other kinds of socialism represented the ascendancy of one understanding of socialist doctrine. Utopian and moralistic traditions were marginalized from the socialist mainstream, diverted into anarchism and syndicalism, or lay in wait to provide the foundation for later revisionist and reformist tendencies. The further development was the extension of Marx's work into a body of scientific socialist doctrine that served for an important period as the integrating ideology of international socialism. During this period socialism assumed for itself the full status of a comprehensive scientific doctrine, not a moral doctrine or modest empirical theory, and presented itself to the world – and the world to itself – in those terms.

This is not the place to explore in any detail the process whereby this development took place. The role of Engels, who tends to get a bad press these days in this respect, is usually identified as central. The words of his famous speech at Marx's graveside set the tone: 'Just as Darwin discovered the law of development of organic nature, so Marx discovered the law of development of human history.' Engels's own work, especially his *Anti-Dühring*, which appeared after Marx's death, came to be accepted as the authoritative frame of reference through which Marx's work was to be viewed. The effect of this was to systematize Marxism into a complete body of scientific knowledge, sustained by a method that was now elevated into a 'dialectical materialism' that was universal in its application, embracing even the natural world itself. Through Engels Marxism was therefore reinforced in its status as a complete and self-contained science of society, while socialism was reinforced in a status independent of moral values because it became rooted in a revealed process of historical determination. In identifying the role of Engels in this systematization of Marxism, it should also be said that he was accurately reflecting a general late-nineteenth-century climate of ideas that was saturated with scientism, positivism, and historicism. It would have been difficult to resist such a climate. In Engels's case, attached as he was to the natural sciences, the task was not to resist this climatic penetration of Marxism but fully to assimilate Marxism to it.

This enterprise proved entirely successful and shaped the presentation of the socialist argument for at least a generation (and, in a sense, for much longer). Although its roots were in Marxism, in its *marxisant* form its influence extended much more widely and penetrated the thinking and assumptions of large numbers of socialists of different kinds. Before looking at some examples of what this involved, it is important to register the general and essential effect of this understanding and presentation of the socialist position. It produced a particular mode of argument, a doctrinaire mode that packaged up socialism into a tight scientific system. In terms of the general development of socialism, there is a real sense in which this mode of argument was more significant than the content of its particular doctrines. In other words, socialists came to believe that they understood the historical process, and that this understanding anchored their political activity in a secure scientific basis. The main elements of this basis are familiar enough (for example, Marx's account of historical stages, the determining role of the mode of production, the fatal contradictions of capitalism, the revolutionary mission of the proletariat), but their combined effect was to enthrone socialism as a complete scientific system, a status that was to be defended against critics and upheld in the face of difficult evidence. A further effect was that any doctrinal developments or innovations (for example, concerning the exact nature of capitalism's collapse, or the analysis of imperialism) had to be presented and claimed as a reinforcement of Marxism's scientific status at points of possible vulnerability, rather than as an erosion of that status in any way.

What this status ensured was the necessary character of the transition from capitalism to socialism. This was, so to speak, the bottom line of scientific socialism. It was an outcome that did not depend upon an act of will or exercises in moral persuasion. Nor was it an outcome that was contingent or merely available. It also involved thinking of the historical process in terms of the succession of one kind of society by another, a process marked by a transitional break-point of some kind. So here was a scientific doctrine that was also a doctrine with political implications in the world of historical action. One important implication was that socialists constantly sought to locate their political activity within the terms of doctrinal orthodoxy, even (or perhaps especially) when such activity seemed to point in contrary directions. Doctrinal orthodoxy guaranteed the success of the activity, or so it was believed, or at least bestowed legitimacy upon it. Something of what this involved in practice will be seen shortly. There is one further general feature of the scientific mode of argument identified here that should be noticed. The belief in doctrinal completeness constantly tempted 'scientific' socialists to reduce and compress evidence into ready-made explanatory categories that left no room for loose ends. This is reflected, as Ralph Miliband once said, in an attitude of mind to which Marxists have been endemically prone: 'This is the belief that because A and B are not *totally* different, they are not *really* different at all.' Yet history has been full of loose ends, and these have posed particular problems for those socialists who believed they had solved its riddles.

This belief was central to pre-1914 socialist orthodoxy in Europe, which is why the events of 1914 produced such a trauma. It was capitalism that was supposed to collapse, not socialist internationalism. Nationalism was supposed to be eclipsed by the forces making for global revolution. There is terrible irony in the fact that it is communism that has collapsed and nationalism that has danced on its grave. The ability of events to inflict such damage on socialist positions (in 1914, and then in 1917) was precisely because socialists had converted Marxism into an allegedly impregnable theoretical system. Thus Karl Kautsky, the Second International's leading theoretician and upholder of doctrinal orthodoxy, had founded Marxism's status upon its historical materialism, which, uniquely, was able to explain how a process of capitalist maturation would usher in the victory of the proletariat and the establishment of socialism. Kautsky hitched Darwinism to Engels's initial codification of Marxism to produce a version of socialism as historical science that unravelled the motor and direction of social development. 'Marxist socialism', he declared, 'is nothing else, in the final analysis, than the science of history with the viewpoint of the proletariat at its point of departure.'

Kautsky is always taken as the symbol of doctrinal orthodoxy in this period, but the more significant point is that his mode of argument, with its emphasis on the essentially scientific character of socialism, was itself a reflection of a prevailing orthodoxy. For example, Rosa Luxemburg, a leading figure on the left wing of German social democracy who maintained a vigorously independent line on a range of questions, was supremely orthodox in her insistence that socialism had to be securely rooted in an analysis that showed it to be objectively necessary. It was this insistence that led her to advance a particular economic analysis (in her theory of accumulation) of the exact conditions and reasons why Marx's general account of capitalist collapse would be vindicated. Her analysis was idiosyncratic in terms of the prevailing Marxist orthodoxy on this matter, but reflected the need to prevent any doubt that socialism could provide a scientific demonstration of the inevitability of capitalism's downfall. More generally, Plekhanov (usually described as the father of Russian Marxism) carried the codification of Marxism still further, expounding and defending its status as a complete philosophical system and presenting it in the form of handbooks or manuals. This was an approach that later characterized the official Marxism that became the state ideology of the Soviet Union. Even where Marx's work was genuinely extended – as it was by the Austro-Marxist Hilferding in his analysis of finance capital and imperialism – to take account of developments in the international economy, its viewpoint and conclusion were still those of an orthodoxy that saw its task as identifying the trends presaging the destruction of capitalism and the victory of the proletariat.

SOCIALISM AND CERTAINTY

So here was a scientific socialism that exhibited great intellectual distinction in its construction of elaborate theoretical systems demonstrating, with the reasons discovered by Marx, why socialism was immanence in history. If the focus here is on the science and the immanence at the expense of the constructs themselves, the reason is that these are the defining characteristics of this kind of socialism. Moreover, its adherents have always wanted to affirm that this is so, whatever their particular disagreements. Thus, Rosa Luxemburg, in the controversy over Bernstein's revisionism, explained why the theory of capitalist collapse was central to scientific socialism, for 'if one admits, with Bernstein, that capitalist development does not move in the direction of its own ruin, then socialism ceases to be objectively necessary'. In the same context, Kautsky wrote that if once the materialistic conception of history and the conception of the proletariat as the motive force of the coming social revolution were abandoned, then I would have to admit that I was through, that my life no longer had any meaning.

It should also be said that scientific socialism was able, over a long period, to command a wide appeal and exercise considerable influence precisely on the basis of its allegedly scientific status. This was recognized by the French syndicalist Sorel, for whom scientific socialism was true only in a pragmatic sense, as an ideological weapon to sustain the proletariat in its revolutionary mission. It would be possible to document the way in which individual socialists have been profoundly influenced by the historical certainties offered by scientific socialism. To take just two examples, both British: William Morris described how he was 'in for a fine pessimistic end of life' until his outlook was transformed by the knowledge that 'the seeds of a great change, what we others call Social Revolution, were beginning to germinate'. Then later John Strachey, the most effective exponent of the communist version of Marxism in the 1930s, described as 'the essential argument in its favour' the fact that it was 'the one method by which human civilisation can be maintained at all'. This line of argument prompted one observer to remark (presciently, in view of Strachey's subsequent renunciation of Marx and embrace of Keynes) that 'one clearly feels that had there been any possibility of preserving the bourgeois system healthy and progressive, Strachey would not have been for changing it'.

If the events of 1914 blew a hole in the immaculate doctrinal structure of Second International socialism and began the process of formal and final rupture within international socialism, the events of 1917 turned the hole into a chasm. In terms of doctrinal orthodoxy, the Bolshevik revolution should not have happened. Instead of a mature capitalism with a developed working class providing the site for socialism, as described by orthodox scientific socialism, here was a revolutionary seizure of power in a peasant society lacking both the political and the economic development that it was the historic task of capitalism to bring about as the basis for socialism. Hence the opposition to Leninism mounted by both Kautsky and Plekhanov, the accepted guardians of Marxist orthodoxy: the economic conditions were wrong, and the revolution could only be sustained by repression.

However, if this judgement was doctrinally correct, and even if it was vindicated by subsequent developments, it was also a reflection on the intrinsic vulnerabilities of scientific socialism that it could find itself so exposed and undermined by historical events. The golden age of scientific socialism had come to an end, and its mantle was now appropriated and deployed as the official ideology of Soviet communism, except that its scientific credentials were now rooted in what became known as Marxism-Leninism.

In many respects it is Lenin who provides the most telling epitaph to the ascendancy and decline of doctrinaire socialism. This is not, as is often claimed, because he was the revolutionary opportunist who drove the bulldozer of practice through the cathedral of theory (or, to put it more plainly, because he was a socialist of the deed and not of the book). Rather, it is because he was precisely the opposite, a supremely doctrinaire socialist who always insisted on hammering out his practice on the anvil of theory (as is emphasized and documented in Neil Harding's study of *Lenin's Political Thought*). The task was to root revolutionary practice in a secure theoretical position. Thus, by 1917 Lenin had satisfied himself that socialist revolution in Russia was authorized by his theory of monopoly capitalism and imperialism, that 'the objective process of development is such that it is impossible to advance from monopolies (and the war has magnified their number, role and importance ten-fold) without advancing towards socialism'. So Lenin was, in Harding's words, 'an extraordinarily doctrinaire politician' whose practical activity represented the relentless application of theoretical positions even when circumstances seemed wholly unpropitious and when he himself was in a minority. Leninism was the culmination of a ⸌ Marxist tradition in which theory was endowed with a predictive quality, able to unravel the *future* course of social development and requiring only that socialist practice should synchronize with it. Lenin's victory was, therefore, the consummation of this tradition and not (as is sometimes claimed) its abrogation. Yet its consummation was also its disintegration, when the theoretical underpinning of Lenin's position (the anticipation of global revolution born out of the havoc wreaked by imperialism) was swept away by the failure of events to behave as theory predicted. Lenin's revolution was rooted in doctrine, not opportunism, but the nature of its success provided a testimony to the disabilities of the whole doctrinal tradition of scientific socialism. The essential point is not, of course, that its theory was wrong, but that it rested upon a fundamental misunderstanding of what theory was and of its role in socialist politics.

Something of this kind was argued by Bernstein, which is why his 'revisionism' was rounded on so ferociously by the orthodox of the Second International. In challenging some of the leading elements of the prevailing Marxist orthodoxy (the theory of value, proletarian impoverishment, class polarization, capitalist collapse) and in suggesting the reformist implications of such revision he was also challenging the entire schematic, scientific basis of that orthodoxy. In terms of the base-superstructure relationship contained in Marx's production theory, Bernstein argued the need to give 'the ideological, and especially the ethical, factors greater space for independent activity than was formerly the case'. Similarly, if economic forces alone could not be relied upon to deliver socialism, then it was necessary in Bernstein's view to construct a separate moral case for socialism. In other words, one kind of socialist doctrine had to be at least complemented by another. This marked an important moment in the development of the modern social democratic tradition, although this development was already apparent in the political practice, if not in the theoretical utterances, of many of those who denounced revisionism so loudly.

It was also apparent in the character of socialist arguments heard outside Germany, the home of Second International orthodoxy. For example, in the case of Jaurès, the leader of French socialism, his adherence to Marxism stopped short of regarding it as a total system and he drew freely upon other traditions. In particular, he presented socialism not merely as a scientific doctrine but as an expression of humanity's long, conscious pursuit of moral values. Beneath the doctrinal umbrella of the Second International, Jaurès and Kautsky therefore represented different kinds of socialism. To Jaurès, socialism was essentially a matter of values; to Kautsky, it was above all else a comprehensive science of society. Then there was British socialism, in which Marxist influence was small and had anyway been countered by a Fabianism that, refusing to feel inferior theoretically to Marxism, claimed to offer in its theory of economic rent an account of capitalist exploitation superior to that of Marx's theory of surplus value; while in its historical analysis it offered an account of the direction of social development (described by Sidney Webb in *Fabian Essays* as 'the irresistible sweep of social tendencies') that provided the basis, at least in England, for a politics of collectivist reform. The first Fabians were not mere empiricists, as is frequently alleged, but confident doctrinaires (though of the kind that did not demand the enforcement of orthodoxy). However, the central and distinguishing fact about British socialism as a whole was that it was imbued with a deep moralism, drawn from a variety of sources. In Tawney's phrase, it was a socialist tradition that was 'unashamedly ethical'. If this isolated it from the world of pre-1914 scientific socialism, when it was relegated to the status of a theoretically primitive poor relation, it later enabled it to play a role in the construction of a democratic socialism upon a different basis. It has some claim to be playing that role again now, in the reconstruction of democratic socialism after the ravages of the neo-liberal revolution from the right.

THE DANGERS OF DOCTRINE

The mode of socialist argument discussed here, with its elevation of theory to the status of scientific doctrine, has carried with it a number of unhelpful consequences for socialist politics. The example of Lenin has already provided one dramatic illustration of such a consequence, but it is possible to identify a range of others, both particular and general. For example, the sort of determinism that conditioned the outlook of the pre-1914 German Social Democratic Party, with its belief in the maturation of capitalism as the necessary prelude to the inevitable victory of the proletariat, proved to be a less than helpful guide to action. It produced an immobilism, a passive waiting for conditions to ripen, that opened up a disabling gulf between the party's revolutionary theory and its actual political practice. Or consider the phenomenon of fellow-travelling, in particular the way in which so many western socialist intellectuals persuaded themselves in the 1930s that Stalinist Russia was a beacon of socialism. Without trying to explore this phenomenon in all its genuine historical complexity, it can at least be said that it reflected the inheritance of a doctrinal tradition which taught that socialism was to be defined in terms of the abolition of private property and the socialization of the means of production, and that therefore the Soviet Union was 'essentially' a socialist society that had to be supported and defended by other socialists (even if this involved glossing over or averting the eyes from causes of disquiet). Indeed, throughout the 1930s socialists reared in a theoretical tradition that promised both the inevitability of capitalist collapse and a historical schema in which socialism was the only successor to capitalism were ill equipped to negotiate that troublesome decade, even when they persuaded themselves (as the widespread appeal of Marxism testified) that they were singularly, indeed uniquely, well equipped in this respect. Their theory left no space for capitalist recovery and stabilization (which is why the reformers of capitalism, especially the social democratic ones, were so derided by their Marxist critics); and their understanding of fascism as essentially the death agony of monopoly capitalism ignored the possibility that it might be necessary to distinguish and even defend capitalist democracy from something worse (instead of coupling fascism with the 'objective' social fascism of the social democrats, as communist doctrine and practice did at one stage). The refusal of the German communists to make common cause against Hitler is a stark reminder that doctrinal traditions carry with them momentous consequences for political action, and inaction, in the real world.

If these are examples of particular consequences, some more general consequences and characteristics associated with the elevation of theory into the role of scientific (or quasi-scientific) doctrine may be identified. A basic but not insignificant point is that since scientific socialism requires scientific socialists, the effect is that advancement of orthodoxy becomes advancement of the bearers of that orthodoxy. Correct doctrine and its proper application are held to be so central to the socialist project that a crucial role is given to the dealers in doctrine, whose superior understanding of the historical process enables them to lead a party that in turn will guide the masses in the appropriate political direction. Kautsky declared: 'Knowledge is still today a privilege of the property-owning classes: the proletariat cannot create out of itself a strong and living socialism. It must have it brought to it.' It will be necessary to return to this matter of 'consciousness from without' at a later stage; but for the moment it is enough to remember that a socialism that defines itself in terms of its possession of scientific knowledge also carries with it a special authority for the possessors of that knowledge. It is an authority that has often been claimed, and converted into power.

There is an even more general, and more fundamental, characteristic associated with the theoretical tradition that claimed to base itself upon Marx's work. Marx advanced a pathbreaking theory of the long-term determinants of social structure and social change, but this was extended by the tradition that took his name into a science of immediate political action. Lichtheim makes this point well, in relation to Marx's class theory:

> This doctrine incorporated a highly original analysis applicable to long-run changes in the economic and social foundations of the political order. It thus provided an important tool for historians and sociologists concerned with the evolution of society since the sixteenth century, but it was useless as a guide to short-term political action.

Not only could it not perform this role, but those who deployed it in this way converted a theory of long-run economic determination into a position that reduced politics to a branch of economics. Such 'reductionism' and 'economism' has always been a central feature of the Marxist tradition, at least until recently. It has also sustained what Frank Parkin has ironically described as 'the Marxist science of predicting the past'.

This suggests a further problem. If a general theory of long-term social change was treated as a handbook of short-term political action, then the model of political economy provided by that theory, in its analysis of the dynamics of capitalism (and here the problem lies with its original formulation as much as with its subsequent use), was also treated as a doctrine of political consequences. In other words, a theory about value, falling profits, capitalist concentration, etc. (which may be more or less valid) was extended into a doctrine about the necessary political and social consequences of that theory (class conflict, consciousness, socialism). Yet this is an illegitimate and misleading extension, since the two domains are analytically distinct. Marx constructed a philosophical bridge between them, not an empirical one, and this bridge has been unable to support the weight of empirical evidence that has pressed down upon it. Even if Marx is acquitted of iron determinism there is *enough* economic determinism in his approach (what Engels was to describe as the '*ultimately* determining element') to leave too little space for the operation of other factors. Yet it is these 'other factors' that have intervened on so many different fronts to prevent Marx's political economy delivering its political consequences. Class-consciousness has taken different forms, within particular societies and between societies, and has produced integration as well as resistance. The 'superstructure' of ideas, beliefs, social groupings, states, religions, ethnicities, nationalisms, etc. has consistently demonstrated a marked reluctance to be determined, and has evidenced a considerable ability to do some determining of its own (an ability that stretched to its economic base, as Stalin demonstrated in practice if not in theory). The point here, then, is not to ask the question why the theoretical model has failed to deliver the political goods (the painful and persistent question of so much Marxism of the recent past), but to identify the flaw in an approach that invited such failure by believing that its theoretical model of capitalism was also a doctrine of political consequences for socialism. It was not, and the fact that it was not revealed its status to be, as Peter Worsley puts it, not a general science of *society* but 'a political economy that stopped short of becoming a sociology'. Or a politics, it might be added. This explains why Marxists continue to produce some of the most acute analysis of the political economy of capitalism, but also why this is now so conspicuously disconnected from any convincing project for socialism. Inverting Marx's famous injunction, their mission is not to change the world but to interpret it.

When democratic socialists have formulated their critique of traditional Marxism, they have wanted to deflate its scientific pretensions. Even when accepting in general terms Marx's account of the centrality of the mode of production and its class basis in explaining historical development and the broad structure of societies, democratic socialists have parted company with any thoroughgoing economic determinism. They have rejected it as in-adequate history, and have wanted to assert a realm of at least partial independence for politics, values, and ideas (a realm that provides the arena for a democratic socialist politics). They have also challenged Marx's account of class polarization, working-class immiserization, and capitalist collapse; and have identified the practical failure of these and other Marxist expectations.

However, beyond these particular issues there are two main lines of criticism. First, there is the effect that Marxism has had upon Marxists: they parrot the texts, reduce everything to rigid economic categories, believe they alone know how societies work, regard Marxism as a total, self-contained system, and exhibit a politics of arrogant intolerance (especially towards other, non-Marxist, socialists who are pityingly accused of 'idealism'). It is argued that these characteristics derive from the scientific status that the

Marxist tradition has, falsely, claimed for itself. They are much less in evidence these days, of course, as this parade of certainties has collapsed, but old habits die hard. The second main line of criticism from democratic socialists has centred on Marxism's lack of an ethical basis; indeed, its repudiation of the need for such a basis. Thus Lenin in 1920:

> We say that our morality is entirely subordinated to the interests of the proletariat's class struggle. . . . Morality is what serves to destroy the old exploiting society and to unite all the working people around the proletariat, which is building up a new, a communist society. . . . To a Communist all morality lies in this united discipline and conscious mass struggle against the exploiters. We do not believe in an eternal morality, and we expose the falseness of all the fables about morality.

This is a polemical statement, but nevertheless represents the rejection of the need for an independent moral basis for socialism that has characterized the Marxist tradition. This position has been attacked by democratic socialists, partly because of the devaluation of the individual implied by the refusal to deal in anything but class categories, but also because of its fusion of the historically necessary and the morally desirable. All socialists might have as their objective a classless society, but there is a fundamental distinction between those who present this objective in terms of a scientific doctrine of historical immanence and those who regard it as a moral doctrine of the good society. Democratic socialists, taking their stand on the latter position, have therefore seen the Marxist tradition as providing an inadequate and unsatisfactory basis for socialism, despite its theoretical grandeur and comprehensive claims. As Bernard Crick has put it, 'theories of socialism without critical moral philosophy are as undesirable as they are impossible'. If the Marxist tradition has provided some of socialism's most sophisticated theoretical analysis, it is the democratic socialist tradition that has best developed its moral doctrine.

It might be said that in some sense this is a historical distinction, not just because of the general fate of the Marxist tradition as a whole but also because of the variety of more recent Marxisms. There is certainly much less Marxist 'science' these days (although it is not so very long since Althusser managed to restore the scientific status of Marx's theory by banishing the empirical world altogether). Marx the 'humanist' has been moved to centre stage, his work presented more modestly as a fruitful method of analysis, and (picking up from the ideas of Antonio Gramsci, Italian Marxist theorist and an early leader of the Italian Communist Party) there has been less economic determinism and more attention to the role of 'superstructural' elements and the importance of human subjectivity. These developments, of course, did not apply to 'official' Marxism, nor to much of Third World Marxism, but they do reflect the changing character of Marxism in the West. They may even reflect a process of integration of Marxism into a broader democratic socialism, something that might have occurred much earlier but for the Bolshevik revolution and is likely to be completed by the demise of those regimes spawned by that revolution. For the moment, though, it is still necessary to identify the different kinds of doctrine that have sustained different kinds of socialism.

Of course, socialism does require both positive doctrine and normative doctrine, empirical theory and moral philosophy. If a socialism without a moral doctrine is impossible, then a socialism without an empirical theory can become a mere fantasy. Yet the conversion of empirical theory into scientific doctrine has produced a contempt for the 'idealism' of a socialism of moral values. Similarly, some versions of 'moral' socialism have carried with them a contempt for theory. Both positions are inadequate, and have proved disabling in practice. However, to say that both kinds of doctrine are required by socialism is not to say that both are of equal status. There is a difference between a tradition that began life by believing (as Marx put it) that it was 'the riddle of history solved, and . . . knows itself to be that solution' and which continued to trade in a superior currency of essentialism, contradictions, and objectivism, and a tradition that offers a moral programme nourished by empirical theory. Perhaps William Morris's reported reply to the questioner who asked accusingly 'Does Comrade Morris accept Marx's Theory of Value?' was an attempt to explain this: 'To speak frankly, I do not know what Marx's Theory of Value is, and I'm damned if I want to know.'

4   Methods

What is generally called the ultimate goal of socialism is nothing to me; the movement is everything.

(Eduard Bernstein)

If socialists have disagreed about the kind of doctrine that socialism essentially is, this disagreement has extended into further differences concerning the means whereby socialist doctrines are to be realized in practice. The two disagreements are closely connected. Thus when the 'revisionists' challenged the orthodoxies of scientific socialism on the matter of the necessary collapse of capitalism, this challenge implied not merely that socialist arguments had to be constructed on a different kind of doctrinal basis but that the strategies and methods employed by socialists had also to be revised.

REFORM AND REVOLUTION

Indeed, this was the political significance of that celebrated dispute to its various protagonists. Revisionism implied reformism, while orthodoxy involved revolution. In fact, matters were not quite as straightforward as this dichotomy suggests, for reasons to be noticed shortly, but it was nevertheless inevitable that arguments about economic doctrine should extend into arguments about political method. If the breakdown of capitalism was just around the corner of history, and if socialism and barbarism were the only alternatives in this situation, then the revolutionary assumption of power by the proletariat was an integral part of the historical prospectus. However, if there was nothing inevitable about capitalism's collapse, if it was capable of stabilization and adjustment, then socialism would need to develop a reformist strategy linking state action and electoral pressure. It is clear from this that arguments about methods do not stand alone but are intimately related to wider socialist positions.

It should also be evident that socialists have argued for, and practised, a variety of methods in pursuit of their objectives. Although this variety is frequently compressed into those familiar categories marked 'reform' and 'revolution', such compression does scant justice to the modalities of these terms, while obscuring from view other dimensions of the argument about methods. It has been possible to be a reformer without also becoming a reformist. There have been revolutionary socialists who have organized for reform, just as there have been non-revolutionary socialists who have sometimes allowed for the possibility of revolution. Parliamentary socialism does not necessarily exclude other, extra-parliamentary, forms of action. Some socialists have rejected violence; others have embraced it. Some have emphasized the need for disciplined organization; others the need for spontaneity. There have been insurrectionists, and revolutionaries who have denounced insurrectionism. Socialists have sought to capture the state, and to destroy it. Political action has been opposed by industrial action. Political action for economic purposes has been matched by industrial action for political purposes. Then there have been those socialists who have sought to point the way forward by constructing experiments in practical socialism within and alongside capitalism.

It is possible to identify these different approaches throughout socialism's history. By the middle of the nineteenth century the main positions, the basis for subsequent traditions, were already in evidence. There was a 'communism' that was revolutionary and insurrectionary, associated with the names of Babeuf and Buonarroti, the extreme left wing of the French Revolution, and which found its continuing expression in the insurrectionary activities of Blanqui and his apostles of revolutionary vanguardism ('Blanquism'). There were 'utopian' socialists who thought that the reform of society could be effected by enlightened legislation and rational legislators (the Saint-Simonian tradition), or who sought, like the Fourierists and Owenites, to found small communities on the basis of their principles of social reconstruction. There were socialists, like Louis Blanc, who laid the basis for a reformism that involved forming alliances and securing parliamentary victories, and which was extended by Lassalle in Germany into a strategy of electoral organization and state action. There were also other socialists, like Proudhon, who in their espousal of direct action by producers nourished anarchist and syndicalist traditions that rejected 'political' socialism and parliamentarism in favour of the self-emancipation of industrial militancy.

When Marx set out to conquer the workers' movement with his ideas, it was against this background of competing strategies. He had to transcend them theoretically, and defeat them practically. What this involved can be seen in a number of ways: for example in his brushing aside of the utopians and his attack on the intellectual poverty of Proudhon, the struggle against

Bakunin and the anarchists, the distancing from the primitiveness of Blanquism, and the repudiation of Lassalle. By the final quarter of the nineteenth century, Marx's ideas had achieved a theoretical supremacy within the workers' movement, and this was converted into a practical supremacy when the German Marxists deployed their Marxism as the organizing ideology of their own movement and then of the Second International. Some aspects of what this involved have been discussed already, but it was clearly of central significance that the main body of the European socialist movement adopted the strategic perspective of Marxism. The developing labour movement required a theoretical underpinning and Marxism supplied it. However, this in turn required that Marxism should demonstrate the much-heralded unity of its theory and practice. When it met the labour movement, its status was not merely that of a theory to be subscribed to, but of a strategy to be acted upon. But what was that strategy?

The history of the Second International period testifies to the difficulties lurking behind that simple question. However, these difficulties cannot be separated from the treatment of socialist methods to be found in Marx's own work. The centrality of revolution in Marx's theory is clear, yet despite its centrality there is no extended discussion of the character of the revolutionary process, and this reflects the general absence of a developed theory of politics. Marx's model of social change had revolution at its centre because it was rooted in a conflict theory of society. It presented society as the scene of a class antagonism that was inevitable and irreconcilable, even when it did not assume the form of open warfare and despite the fact that it was wrapped around with layers of ideological mystification. Marx's production theory of society made class conflict the motor of social change, a motor that worked through revolutions (of more or less violence). The revolutionary 'communism' of the early Marx, as expressed in the call to arms of the *Manifesto*, might give way to the long-term structural perspectives of the later Marx, as seen in the *Grundrisse*, where the revolutionary agency slips from view but revolution as the method of social change remains constant and integral.

However, this still leaves open the question of what Marx actually understood by revolution. Some help here may be derived from the obstetric imagery he frequently employed when discussing the transition from one form of society to another. This is the imagery of wombs, embryos and midwives, in which new societies are born out of old ones after a suitable period of gestation and through the agency of an appropriately qualified midwife. Societies are in a condition of perpetual pregnancy, giving birth when they come to ripeness (the exception being socialism, of course, which represented the final discovery of an effective method of social contraception). This imagery does reflect an account of social change that turns on the developing relationship between the forces and relations of production, and in which productive 'fetters' have to be broken when new societies are born. What this meant was that revolution was as inevitable and necessary as childbirth but was likewise to be understood as one moment in a larger and longer process. It was the moment of 'break', when the new was created out of the old, but was to be seen as the culmination of a whole process of social formation. Like childbirth, it was likely to be a painful moment, but it was the pain of transcendence and release.

At risk of exhausting the imagery, Marx's understanding of revolution also carried with it a warning of the dangers of prematurity. If social revolutions were to be understood as one moment in a process of social development, it was unscientific to believe that they could be precipitated in situations where the necessary conditions did not exist or were undeveloped. This was Marx's charge against the insurrectionism of the Blanquists, those 'alchemists of revolution' who believed that 'the only condition for the revolution is a sufficient organisation of their own conspiracy'. According to Engels, the Blanquists believed 'in the principle that revolutions do not make themselves, but are made; that they are made by a comparatively small minority and according to a previously designed plan; and finally, that the time is always ripe'. However, even such warnings against the revolutionary alchemism of unscientific quacks do not serve fully to identify Marx's own position.

If revolution, properly understood, was the motor of social change in Marx's general theory, this did not prevent him from supporting demands for particular social reforms within the existing order or from attaching himself to the cause of democratic republics founded upon universal suffrage. The perspective, however, remained tactical, turning on the relationship between social and democratic reform and the longer-term process of class conflict and revolution. It was a perspective that was decisively influenced by Marx's analysis of the state, an analysis that combined an essentialist position ('merely the organised power of one class for oppressing another') in terms of his general theory with a series of modifications and qualifications in relation to particular state forms. This combination again reflected the absence of a developed theory of politics (and explains why later Marxists have had to spend so much time and energy trying to construct one). The result, in terms of political method, was that Marx presented violent revolution as the model of social change (in the words of *Capital*, 'force is the midwife of every old society pregnant with a new one'), but at the same time, in the *obiter dicta* of his maturity, seemed to allow the possibility that a route of peaceful constitutionalism might be available to the working class in some countries. The most celebrated of such *obiter dicta* is Marx's reported speech in Amsterdam in 1872:

We know of the allowances we must make for the institutions, customs and traditions of the various countries; and we do not deny that there are countries such as America, England, and I would add Holland if I knew your institutions better, where the working people may achieve their goal by peaceful means. If that is true, we must also recognise that in most of the continental countries it is force that will have to be the lever of our revolutions.

Even this brief sketch of Marx's approach is enough to reveal that it provided a profoundly ambiguous legacy. It offered an account of the state as essentially a class agency, yet was accompanied by accounts of actual states that suggested the difficulties with such essentialism. It demonstrated the need for the workers' movement to destroy the state, but also explored the tactics for using it. It announced the necessity of forceful revolution, but also introduced a doctrine of exceptionalism. When combined with the areas of crucial neglect (for example, the role of parties, their relation to classes, the nature of political leadership), this was an elusive political methodology and an ambivalent inheritance. When further combined, as the next chapter shows, with the absence of any sustained discussion of the political structure of socialist society, it became an even more elusive guide to socialist politics. All this may be regarded as a necessary and unsurprising consequence of a theoretical position that, when the relevant qualifications have been registered, gave a secondary and derivative status to politics. However, it also meant that when the meaning of 'revolution' was debated during the Second International period, or when Lenin argued the need to 'smash' the state as good Marxist orthodoxy, it was possible to conscript Marx into competing positions on the battle lines.

REVISIONISTS AND LENINISTS

It was against this background that the 'revolution versus reform' controversy within German Social Democracy took shape. Here was a Marxist party (its Marxism given popular form in its 1891 Erfurt Programme) committed to a revolutionary doctrine but engaged in the electoral and parliamentary politics of reform. This story is usually told in terms of the dangerous, and ultimately fatal, gulf between theory and practice that this involved (a gulf down which European socialism was to fall in 1914). While such a story is clearly true, there are disputes about who its villains are and what alternative endings were available. Lenin, of course, was to use the experience as an object-lesson in the rottenness of European social democracy, revealed as essentially reformist behind its cloak of revolutionary rhetoric, and therefore to be opposed by a genuinely revolutionary communism. However, this was a retrospective discovery on Lenin's part, signalled by his invention of the 'renegade' Kautsky. During the heyday of the Second International Lenin had bowed before the authority of Kautsky as the defender of a correct Marxist revolutionary line against both reformists and insurrectionists, a strategic perspective which was rooted in a scientific understanding of the laws of social development. As Kautsky had put it:

> The task of Social Democracy consists, not in bringing about the inevitable catastrophe, but in delaying it as long as possible, that is to say, in avoiding with care anything that could resemble a provocation or the appearance of a provocation.

In *The Road to Power* (1909) Kautsky had distinguished, as the leading theorist of scientific socialism, between a revolutionary party and a revolution-making party:

> Social democracy is a revolutionary party, but not a revolution-making party. We know that our objective can only be reached through revolution. But we also know that it is no more in our power to make this revolution than it is in the power of our enemies to prevent it. We have no wish either to stir up revolution or to prepare the ground for one.

Such formulations may now, with hindsight, appear to give the game away, reducing revolution to a metaphor and providing a rhetorical camouflage for political passivity, but it should also be remembered how accurately they reflected the doctrinal atmosphere of Second International scientific social-ism. This involved waiting for the maturation of capitalism, which, in turn, would inevitably deliver socialism. There would necessarily be a revolu-tionary moment, but it was the evolutionary process at work that really mattered for it was this that would ensure that when the revolutionary 'break' came the balance of forces would be such as to guarantee a swift and painless victory. From this perspective, then, it was perfectly possible, indeed necessary, to be both reformer and revolutionary.

In fact, of course, it meant that one was neither a coherent reformer nor a coherent revolutionary. To be the former would have involved thinking through the implications of an electoral road to socialism, while to be the latter would have involved some consideration of how 'maturity' was to be judged and how revolutionary consciousness and activity were to be actively promoted in order to connect with the maturing conditions. This dilemma, and the need for a clear choice of strategy, was perceived in their sharply different ways by both the 'revisionist' Bernstein and the 'radical' Luxem-burg. In challenging the scientific status of key elements of Marxist doctrine, and therefore also their inevitabilist implications, Bernstein argued for a view of socialism as a process that was already underway and could be carried forward indefinitely by democratic reformism. In 1898 he wrote:

> It is my firm conviction that the present generation will already see realised a large part of socialism, if not in official form, at least in content. The constant enlargement of social duties, i.e. of the duties and corresponding rights of the individual against society and of the duties of society to the individual, the extension of the right of society, as organised in the nation or the state, to supervise economic life, the construction of democratic self-government at village, district and provincial levels, and the extension of the tasks of these associations – and that for me is development towards socialism.

It was in this sense that Bernstein, anticipating a fundamental theme of twentieth century social democracy, could declare that for him the 'ultimate goal' of socialism was nothing and the 'movement' everything. Building socialism was a continuous process, not a single, dramatic cataclysm.

Bernstein's view was met with a chorus of denunciation from the guardians of Marxist orthodoxy. Perhaps this really derived from a sense that Bernstein had simply theorized the practice of the Social Democrats, confronting them with the fact that they were in reality a party of reform even if they remained formally attached to a doctrine of revolution. Even Engels, in his much discussed preface to a new edition of Marx's *Class Struggles in France*, which he wrote in 1895 not long before his death, seemed to have provided a decisive endorsement of the constitutional road. Declaring that 'the mode of struggle of 1848 is today obsolete from every point of view', Engels proclaimed the advantages of electoral politics and eulogized the advance of German Social Democracy as a model for others:

> Its growth proceeds as spontaneously, as steadily, as irresistibly, and at the same time as tranquilly as a natural process. All government interventions have proved powerless against it. We can count even today on two and a half million voters. If it continues in this fashion, by the end of the century we shall conquer the greater part of the middle section of society, petty bourgeois and small peasants, and grow into the decisive power in the land, before which all other powers will have to bow, whether they like it or not. To keep this growth going without interruption until of itself it gets beyond the control of the ruling governmental system, not to fritter away this daily increasing shock force in advance guard fighting, but to keep it intact until the day of the decision, that is our main task. . . . The irony of world history turns everything upside down. We, the 'revolutionaries', the 'rebels' – we are thriving far better on legal methods than on illegal methods and revolt. The parties of order, as they

call themselves, are perishing under the legal conditions created by themselves.

The ambiguity remained (there would still be 'the day of the decision', and the party of order would throw over legalism when this became necessary), but Engels had clearly extended Marx's allowance of particular exceptions to the revolutionary norm into a general vindication of constitutional politics as the appropriate socialist method at the end of the nineteenth century. This was not a theoretical discovery, but a recognition of the actual role that mass socialist parties were then playing in the political life of Western European societies. They were framing practical programmes of reform and campaigning for electoral support on the basis of them. As Bebel, the German SPD leader, expressed it: 'The heart of the people turns towards us because we take up the cause of their daily needs.' Here was a process of integration into 'normal' politics that could not easily be combined with a continuing commitment to overthrowing the political system itself. How far such integration could go was thrown into sharp relief in France in 1898, when a socialist accepted ministerial office in a bourgeois government; and this 'Millerand case' sent shock waves through international socialism. In general terms, it looked increasingly implausible that, in a theoretical sense, a tactic of reform was organically connected to a strategy of revolution. As Joll comments in his history of the Second International, 'It is very hard to work for the overthrow of existing society if one is stopping by the way to improve the drainage system or the transport service.'

There were those who, like Bernstein, recognized the developing gap between revolutionary theory and reformist practice within social democracy but, unlike Bernstein, sought to close the gap by amending the practice in the direction of the theory. This was the position of the radical left wing of German social democracy, represented pre-eminently by Rosa Luxemburg; and of the equivalent wing of the Second International itself, represented above all by Lenin. Both Luxemburg and Lenin fell in behind Kautsky in his rebuttal of revisionism and later they were both to mount attacks on the leadership of social democracy; but also on each other. Luxemburg's *Social Reform or Revolution* (1899) was a sustained polemic against Bernstein's revisionism and its reformist implications, and an assertion of the view that reforms had no value or meaning except as part of a strategy of revolution. There could be no legal route to socialism because the domination of capital was essentially an extra-legal phenomenon. Thus reform and revolution were 'not different methods of historic development that can be picked out at pleasure from the counter of history, just as one chooses hot or cold sausages', but represented different kinds of activity with intrinsically different objectives:

That is why people who pronounce themselves in favour of the method of legislative reform *in place* of and in *contradistinction* to the conquest of political power and social revolution, do not really choose a more tranquil, calmer and slower road to the *same* goal, but a *different* goal. Instead of taking a stand for the establishment of a new society, they take a stand for surface modifications of the old society. If we follow the political conceptions of revisionism, we arrive at the same conclusion that is reached when we follow the economic theories of revisionism. Our programme becomes not the realisation of *socialism*, but the reform of *capitalism*; not the suppression of the system of wage labour, but the diminution of exploitation, that is, the suppression of the abuses of capitalism instead of the suppression of capitalism itself.

Luxemburg's attack on the theoretical revisionism of Bernstein later extended into an assault on the practical reformism of the SPD leadership. Having a profound belief in the revolutionary potential of the working class, she berated a political style that stifled the development of revolutionary consciousness rather than actively promoted it. Her advocacy of the mass strike as a political weapon, a lesson she drew from the events of 1905 in Russia, epitomized her belief in the 'spontaneity' of proletarian self-emancipation. Following Marx, Luxemburg believed that the proletariat could and would emancipate itself through a genuine revolution of the masses. On the one hand, this led her into opposition to the revisionists and centrists of social democracy, but it also involved a rejection of the Leninist organizational model of revolution that turned on the role of the vanguard party. Instead of a dynamic and 'dialectical' relationship between party and class, leaders and masses, Leninism represented 'a mechanical transfer of the organisational principles of the Blanquistic movement of conspiratorial groups to the Social Democratic movement of the working masses'.

Where Luxemburg and Lenin were in agreement was in their attribution of responsibility for the socialist debacle of 1914 to the leadership of the social democratic movement. They both believed that revolutions had to be made (albeit in rather different ways) not waited for, and their charge against the pre-1914 social democratic leadership was that it played a waiting game that both concealed its actual relapse into reformism and atrophied the working-class movement. Just as Kautsky had been able to draw upon a reading of Marx to sustain an evolutionary perspective of maturation and ripeness in which revolution as activity faded from view, so Lenin was able (notably in his *State and Revolution*, written on the eve of the Bolshevik revolution) to draw with no less credibility upon an alternative reading in which the transition to socialism took the form of a revolutionary push in which states were smashed, oppositions crushed, and political violence liberally deployed. There could be no truck with the fraud of parliamentary democracy:

> To decide once every few years which member of the ruling class is to repress and crush the people through parliament – this is the real essence of bourgeois parliamentarism, not only in parliamentary-constitutional monarchies, but also in the most democratic republics.

Revolution was on the socialist agenda, no longer as a metaphor, and as the only item.

Lenin had satisfied himself, as seen in the previous chapter, that the objective conditions for global revolution had been established and so set about the business of lighting the Russian spark. His success in this task, on the basis of the organizational principles he hammered out, later provided the foundation for the (communist) claim that Leninism represented the extension of Marxism into the age of revolution (an extension that came to be sanctified as 'Marxism-Leninism'). In essence, the claim was – and in some quarters perhaps still is – that Leninists are professionals in the business of revolution-making. It was this professionalism that was supposed to have been passed on to the communist parties that were established throughout Europe by the Third International, with the task of saving the working class of these countries from the degeneracy of social democracy and providing them with revolutionary leadership. When the international revolution failed to materialize (despite a number of revolutionary outbreaks in the immediate post-1918 period, and a widespread panic among European governments about the contaminating spread of Bolshevism), socialism was left in its disabling state of polarization between a 'revolutionary' communism and a 'reformist' social democracy.

Perhaps two footnotes to the account of pre-1914 social democracy should be entered. The first concerns syndicalism; the second relates to British socialism. The former rejected the whole business of bourgeois parliamentarism and political action in favour of direct action by the producers. The latter was overwhelmingly parliamentary and constitutionalist. Both addressed themselves to the matter of reformism: one to denounce it, the other to embrace it. The French syndicalist philosopher Georges Sorel was preoccupied with the debilitating effect of parliamentarism on working-class militancy, in its encouragement of ideas of compromise and social peace ('the reconciliation of contraries in the equivocations of the professors'). The need was to promote working-class violence, heroism, and authenticity if the class was to perform its conquering role, and this was to be effected by means of the general strike, the heroic 'myth' of the proletariat. Its function was not to win particular victories, but to clarify, mobilize, and polarize: 'the idea of the general strike has such power behind it that it drags into the revolutionary track everything it touches.' Even though it would be misleading to present Sorel as the representative theorist of syndicalism, the advocacy and practice of producer militancy as an alternative to 'political' socialism continued to provide a minority answer to the question of socialist method. The strategy of 'encroaching control' in industry advocated by the guild socialists in Britain may be seen as one version of this general approach.

If syndicalism stood outside the mainstream of Second International scientific socialism, then so too, in a sharply different way, did British socialism as a whole. Both the moralism of the ethical socialists and the rationalism of the Fabians reinforced the commitment to constitutionalism. The ethical socialists rejected any resort to violence and addressed themselves to moral persuasion and parliamentary agitation. As Keir Hardie frequently expressed it, they were waging war not upon a class but upon a system. Meanwhile, the Fabians were confidently demonstrating (on grounds that seem to have influenced Bernstein) why revolution was unnecessary and why a process of reform that was already well underway could gradually transform capitalist individualism into socialist collectivism. Concluding his contribution to *Fabian Essays* on 'The Transition to Social Democracy', Bernard Shaw reviewed the character of 'the humdrum programme of the practical Social Democrat today' and announced:

> There is not one new item in it. All are applications of principles already admitted, and extensions of practices already in full activity. All have on them that stamp of the vestry which is so congenial to the British mind. None of them compel the use of the words Socialism or Revolution: at no point do they involve guillotining, declaring the Rights of Man, swearing on the altar of the country, or anything else that is supposed to be essentially un-English. And they are all sure to come – landmarks on our course already visible to far-sighted politicians even of the party which dreads them.

It was not necessary to admire this 'sordid, slow, reluctant, cowardly path to justice' with its 'paltry instalments of betterment'; but it was necessary to accept that it had rendered obsolete an earlier socialist catastrophism. In less Shavian form, and with only fleeting interludes of doubt, this became the orthodoxy of twentieth-century social democracy.

STRATEGY MEETS EXPERIENCE

Having mapped out some of the leading positions on the matter of socialist methods that had staked their claim by the fateful second decade of the twentieth century, it is now possible to offer some observations in the light of subsequent experience. It is difficult to avoid the conclusion that each strategy has failed to deliver the goods, at least in the ways so confidently envisaged. The Kautskian perspective of capitalist maturation reaching the point at which socialism would step into its place could scarcely account for the continuance of a chronic overripeness. The Leninist perspective of global revolution had its doctrinal basis cut away the day after it was born, and in its practical application failed to deliver revolution anywhere in Western Europe. The reformist perspective has certainly been able to win power and deliver reforms, in places such as Scandinavia over long and uninterrupted periods, but it has nowhere been able to deliver what any of its assorted pre-1914 protagonists would have regarded as socialism. Syndicalism and its derivatives expired as an effective movement in the aftermath of the First World War. To complete the picture, the polarization that was enforced upon the labour movement not only weakened it, but also closed off options of theory and strategy that might have been available to it.

The murder of Rosa Luxemburg in 1919 symbolized the closure of a non-Leninist revolutionary option (whether or not this was a viable option, when separated from the belief in an essentially revolutionary proletariat, is another matter). The Bolshevik appropriation of Marxism ossified it as a body of theory and, for at least a generation, effectively closed it off as a creative source of socialist strategy. In its communist version, it became an instrument whereby Moscow sought to dress up its line to its satellite parties in the legitimating cloak of scientific socialist doctrine (all the more necessary when this line was so manifestly inappropriate to the domestic situations these parties faced, and when the line was quite likely to be reversed overnight). On the non-communist side, the need to withstand the attacks from the communists pushed many socialists into a narrower and less adventurous form of social democracy than they might otherwise have wished; but in conditions of polarization they had nowhere else to go. Since 1945 some revision in this picture has become necessary, but not of a kind to alter its basic shape, at least not until the continuing fallout from the events of 1989.

A revolutionary socialism chalked up some successes, but in places, forms, and methods a million miles away from the revolutionary prospectus offered by classical Marxism. This remained true in spite of the mobilization of Marxism as revolutionary ideology and the deployment of Leninism as a revolutionary manual. Lenin's demonstration that socialists could make revolutions in unlikely places, given sufficient discipline and organization, stood confirmed. But could they make them in likely places, in the heartlands of developed capitalism, as the classical Marxist tradition envisaged? Here the story since 1945 looks entirely different. Not only did social democracy become more securely reformist in this period (symbolized by the revised doctrinal basis adopted by the German SPD in 1959 at Bad Godesberg), but more secure on the Left. Moreover, there was a striking development in the character of Western European communism in this period. Lenin had blamed the failure of European revolution on the reformism of social democratic leaders, and had established communist parties that would give the working classes of Europe an authentic revolutionary leadership. It became an axiom of the communist tradition that reformist social democracy, in the form of leaders who betrayed their class and were wedded to bourgeois parliamentarism, was the chief obstacle to revolution in the West.

Yet the evolution of communist parties in Western Europe in the generation before the collapse of communism in the East (most notably in Italy, most slowly in France) was precisely in the direction of reformism and constitutionalism, carrying with it a disavowal of any revolutionary intent. Moreover, this stance of 'Eurocommunism' was presented not as a device to avoid frightening the children (i.e. the electors), but as a positive commitment to the political institutions of bourgeois democracy. As Carrillo, the Spanish communist theorist of this new revisionism, put it, 'the political system established in Western Europe, based on representative political institutions – parliament, political and philosophical pluralism, the theory of the separation of powers, decentralisation, human rights, etc. – . . . is in essentials valid'. Eurocommunists would respect this 'essential validity' both in their pursuit of political power and in their exercise of it. All this was clearly a long way from Leninism, and from the role assigned to these parties by Lenin. It was also very close to social democracy, as the left-wing critics of Eurocommunism liked to point out (to one such critic, Ernest Mandel, it was 'incontestable . . . that Eurocommunism today is repeating the reasoning of social democracy yesterday word for word'). Of course, this was strenuously denied by the Eurocommunists, as with Carrillo's distinction between a Eurocommunism that aimed to 'transform' capitalism and a social democracy that merely wanted to 'administer' it. It was argued that there were different kinds of reformism, a kind that meant business and a kind that did not, even though they might look similar. The difference lay in the fact (as Miliband explains in his account of *Marxism and Politics*) that 'on any realistic view' the leaders of social democracy must be 'reckoned as forming part, and a very important part, of the conservative forces of advanced capitalist countries'. Thus, the embarrassment caused by the existence of rival reformisms, Marxist and social democratic, was overcome once it was understood that, objectively speaking, social democrats were really playing for the other side. At least some things in the Marxist universe remained the same.

However, there were also other problems raised by the new tendencies.

Why was the political structure of western democracy to be regarded as 'valid' now, when its invalidity from a Marxist perspective had been proclaimed for so long? Why had revolution become unnecessary, when its indispensability at some point was traditionally regarded as axiomatic? In pondering such questions, it should be recalled that in the Marxist tradition the issue of socialist methods in relation to reformism, parliamentary action, etc. has presented itself as a problem of *tactics*. In other words, the political apparatus of capitalist democracy had no intrinsic merit except in so far as it might offer new tactical opportunities for Marxist strategists. Indeed, its absence of intrinsic merit was an article of faith, and Marxists were constantly stripping off its sham democratic veneer to reveal the class oppression just underneath (as with Arthur Scargill's claim during the 1984–5 miners' strike that the activities of the police clearly revealed how behind its democratic facade Britain was 'really' a police state). Marxist discussion turned on the extent to which bourgeois parliamentarism could be used for socialist purposes. It was in this spirit that Marx had discussed the matter, and that the discussion continued thereafter (including, for example, Lenin's polemic in 1920 against ultra-left anti-parliamentarism in his *'Left-Wing' Communism – An Infantile Disorder*). Against this background the Eurocommunist discovery of the 'validity' of western democracy represented a departure – although to some it looked rather belated and grudging, while to others its significance as a conversion was somewhat devalued by the extent to which it still looked suspiciously like a tactical response. This chapter of contemporary history already feels like a different age.

DEMOCRACY AND SOCIALISM

The twin discoveries that there were different kinds of reformism and that western democracy was valuable in itself could scarcely come as a revelation to democratic socialists. They had been advancing these positions, from within the social democratic tradition, for at least half a century. It was possible for pre-1914 social democracy to assume that socialism would extend and incorporate the inheritance of liberal democracy into its own structures, for this was built into its developmental model of social change. This assumption was no longer possible after 1917, which meant that liberal democracy had either to be denounced as a fraud (as it was by the communists) or embraced as a value (as it was by the social democrats). If 'social democracy' now came to mean a clearly reformist position, whether used in a pejorative or approbatory sense, it also came to signify to its adherents a policy of completing democracy by extending it from the political and civic sphere into the social and economic. In its existing form it was not hollow, as the Marxists tended to argue, but incomplete. Similarly, the term 'democratic socialism' was coined to describe a position that was committed to socialism, but was also committed to democracy as both the method of change and the structural form of socialist society. During the twentieth century it became important for some socialists at least to make such matters clear.

Bolshevism demonstrated that it was perfectly possible for socialism to be undemocratic; while fascism demonstrated that it was equally possible for capitalist democracy to turn into something infinitely worse. The range of historical options therefore expanded beyond the neat categories of pre-1914 scientific socialism. This caused democratic socialists to define their relationship, at least in respect of their own societies, to the inheritance of liberal democracy. This inheritance was to be regarded as a considerable achievement, and socialism was to be regarded as a further development of the same civilizing tradition. Further, this was not merely a matter of political theory but a reflection of the growth and diffusion of a democratic political culture. R. H. Tawney, writing in the 1930s, identified what a political culture 'steeped for two centuries in a liberal tradition' meant for socialism in Britain:

> The result is the existence of a body of opinion, larger, probably, than in most other countries, which is sensitive on such subjects as personal liberty, freedom of speech and meeting, tolerance, the exclusion of violence from politics, parliamentary government – what, broadly, it regards as fair play and the guarantees for it. The only version of socialism which, as things are today, has the smallest chance of winning mass support, is one which accepts that position. Its exponents must realise that the class which is the victim of economic exploitation, instead of merely reading about it, is precisely the class which attaches most importance to these elementary decencies. They must face the fact that, if the public, and particularly the working-class public, is confronted with the choice between capitalist democracy, with all its nauseous insincerities, and undemocratic socialism, it will choose the former every time. They must make it clear beyond the possibility of doubt that the socialist common-wealth which they preach will be built on democratic foundations. That fact is a proof, not of stupidity, but of intelligence. It means that Henry Dubb has the sense to prefer two good things to one. . . . In becoming a socialist, he has no intention of surrendering his rights as a citizen, which after all, he once fought pretty hard to win. But, whether admirable or regrettable, that mentality remains a fact. Any realist strategy must be based upon it.

Tawney's point, it should be noticed, was not merely that it was tactically necessary to take account of the views of Henry Dubb, but that Henry Dubb was right. However, adopting a position of this kind did not also require that democratic socialists should become political innocents. The method to which they committed themselves was only advanced as appropriate to those societies with a tradition and practice of political democracy. Where democracy did not exist, or was flouted, then other methods became available. In particular, if a democratic socialist government found itself subverted by unconstitutional opposition, then it would be fully entitled to answer in kind. The fear, or even expectation, of such subversion was widely expressed and debated on the British Left in the 1930s (so much so that in 1932 the impeccably moderate Clement Attlee, future prime minister, was to be found suggesting that socialists should train people to take over command positions in the armed forces in anticipation of such an eventuality). The ability of the 1945 Labour Government to fulfil its programme could therefore be regarded as a vindication of the viability of a democratic socialist strategy (in G. D. H. Cole's phrase, the answer to the Marxists was now 'in the facts'). However, there was no more reason for democratic socialists than for Marxists to be surprised that a democratically elected Marxist government should be ousted by a coup (as in Chile) or that the prospect of a socialist party coming to power in a general election should be pre-empted by a military takeover (as happened in Greece).

If democratic socialists could regard themselves as having a rather more durable claim to the title than the postwar breed of 'democratic' communists, or than the assorted sects and factions that waged war on social democracy in the name of ideological purity, they also know a thing or two about the varieties of reformism. In its reaction against communism, and its firm embrace of liberal democracy, social democracy has certainly been prone to slacken its socialist resolve. The history of this tendency is there to be seen in both its theoretical development and its exercise of office. It has frequently shown a capacity for degeneration into mere electoralism and governmentalism, making it implausible to claim, except in a rhetorical sense, that its reforming endeavours were part of a wider strategy of social transformation. However, this is not enough to sustain the charge that social democracy is in a generic sense, always and everywhere, a support for capitalism rather than a democratic challenge to it (unless, that is, a mode of analysis is employed in which this is necessarily the case). The historical evidence suggests that social democracy has taken different forms and been capable of delivering different results. It has not delivered 'socialism' of course, but it may be that the time perspective in which such delivery was traditionally envisaged was flawed and that a socialism of process (in Bernstein's sense) requires a different kind of valuation. It may simply be a case of going on going on, even when – as in recent times – circumstances are unpropitious.

However, if this is so, then it requires a clear sense of direction and strategy or it does issue in *mere* reformism and accommodative integration. Here again those democratic socialists who have constituted the left wing of social democracy could reasonably claim to have kept this perspective alive most consistently. Moreover, their advocacy of the democratic method has been coupled with a vigorous and expansive sense of what this involves in terms of political action. It means, as Tawney put it, thinking of democracy not merely as a political mechanism but as 'a force to be released'. It does not mean a retreat into a political passivity, but requires the mobilization of a people. Thus while a Marxist might, like Miliband, attend to the 'considerable constraints' imposed on revolutionary movements by bourgeois constitutionalism, a democratic socialist like Aneurin Bevan emphasizes the tremendous opportunities offered by parliamentary democracy for socialist political action. However, these opportunities have to be exploited to the full, through relentless democratic energy, or vacillation and lassitude will result. In Bevan's words, 'audacity is the mood that should prevail among Socialists as they apply the full armament of democratic values to the problems of the times'. In other words, democratic socialism gives a particular importance to the character and quality of political action; which may explain why Marxists have traditionally regarded this position and its practitioners with such theoretical pity.

There is a final general point here, arising out of these remarks on democratic socialism. It concerns the relationship between socialist means and ends. Democratic socialism, as was seen, contains an argument about both socialist means and socialist ends, and the necessary relationship between them. It is possible, as has also been seen, to take a rather different view of this matter, whereby the choice of means is regarded instrumentally and tactically, and where (for example, with Lenin) it becomes perfectly possible to combine a belief in revolution effected by means of the iron discipline of a vanguard party with a post-revolutionary prospectus of stateless democracy. Such a disassociation of political means and ends not only seems unlikely, but also has all the weight of historical evidence against it. In other words, it is the case not only that political means and ends *should* be related, but also that they *are*. If parliamentary constitutional socialism has (so far) only produced social democracy, then revolutionary socialism has (so far) only produced state authoritarianism. Rosa Luxemburg was clearly right: socialist methods cannot be freely chosen – like hot or cold sausages – from the counter of history. The menu you choose does affect the sort of meal you are likely to get.

5   Structures

To my mind, there have always been two fundamental cleavages in socialist thought – the cleavage between revolutionaries and reformists, and the cleavage between centralisers and federalists.

(G. D. H. Cole)

If the antagonism between reform and revolution is a familiar theme in the history of socialism, the same is not true of the arguments about the structural form of socialism. These arguments have tended in the past to be reduced to accounts of the distracting difficulties caused to mainstream socialism at various periods by the activities of anarchists and syndicalists. Yet, at the end of the twentieth century, questions concerning the structural principles and shape of socialism are once again at the centre of socialist discussion. This suggests the need to identify some of the arguments, issues, and traditions.

SOCIALISM AND STATISM

It may help to clear some ground if the chief reasons for the contemporary interest in these matters are frankly acknowledged. In his magisterial account of the development of Marxism, Kolakowski remarks on 'the strange fate of an idea which began in Promethean humanism and culminated in the monstrous tyranny of Stalin'. Leaving aside (at least for the moment) the implied derivation of Stalin from Marx, this remark may be extended to socialism as a whole. Early-nineteenth-century socialism was, in its various forms, libertarian, democratic, communitarian, and self-managing. These forms are represented by Proudhon's mutualism, Fourier's *phalanstères*, the Owenite experiments in cooperative living, the Saint-Simonian substitution of the administration of things by producers for the government of men by politicians, and, of course, by the comprehensive prospectus for human emancipation offered by Marx. By contrast, late-twentieth-century socialism had come to be associated on all sides with centralism and statism.

This association might be seen as relatively benign (liberal social democracy) or as positively malign (authoritarian communism), but either way the association was there. Twentieth-century communism had invented the monolithic party dictatorship as the organizational model of socialism. Twentieth-century social democracy, through its chosen method of piling ever more powers and responsibilities upon the state, has been the architect of the modern bureaucratic welfare state. Both roads have clearly led socialism a long way from that original vision of a stateless communism. By the 1940s, Schumpeter could declare (in his *Capitalism, Socialism and Democracy*) that 'what may be termed Centralist Socialism seems to me to hold the field so clearly that it would be a waste of space to consider other forms'. These 'other forms' were now judged to have become historically, and technologically, obsolete, with the advocates of a non-statist, associational socialism shunted to the political sidelines. One such advocate was G. D. H. Cole, who concluded his vast survey of the *History of Socialist Thought* at the end of the 1950s with the lonely affirmation that he was 'neither a Communist nor a Social Democrat, because I regard both as creeds of centralisation and bureaucracy'.

A generation later, though, both the radical Right and the radical Left seemed united in their aversion to the state. However, while the Right had a clear sense of what the displacement of the state involved (for example, in terms of deregulation, denationalization, private markets in welfare, more freedom to become unequal) and what it did not involve (above all, any reduction in the political power of the central state, but rather the intensification of such power), the Left seemed to encounter greater difficulties in giving content to an alternative version of socialism. Unlike the Right, it was prepared to curtail the state's political power in the name of democratic accountability and civil liberty, but found it much more difficult to develop a non-centralist version of a socialist economy. It is significant that, at the end of the twentieth century, traditional state socialism seems to have few friends on the contemporary Left in the West; but it is equally significant that the shape of an alternative form of socialism remains elusive, both theoretically and practically.

Some of the reasons for the development of socialism-as-statism can be briefly identified. These range from the particular circumstances in which the world's first socialist revolution took place, a revolution of backwardness organized by a disciplined party, to the reforming ambitions of social democratic parties. The former produced an organizational model of socialism as an authoritarian state bureaucracy rooted in a single party, a model that was to be imposed in some places and adopted in others where socialism presented itself as an agency for nation building and economic development. The latter produced an organizational model of socialism rooted in the increasingly bureaucratized social democratic parties (the oligarchic character of which had been identified early in the century with reference to the German party by Michels in his *Political Parties*), whose central activity has been to press more functions and responsibilities upon an expanding state in the cause of economic and social welfare, but without giving much thought to the consequences of this activity in terms of the organization of an enlarged state or wider socialist objectives.

If these are arguments from practice relevant to the development of socialist statism, there are also of course some important arguments from theory. As was seen earlier, there is a major tradition of organizational socialism, the main thrust of which has been to indict capitalism for the waste and inefficiency consequent upon the anarchy of competition and to counterpose this with the merits of socialist planning. It is clear that the planning argument encompasses a number of themes basic to the socialist position, and equally clear that it is an argument that carries with it a strong centralist bias and an antipathy to a diversity of economic and social initiatives. In his *Farewell to the Working Class*, André Gorz makes this point well:

> The source of the theoretical superiority of socialism over capitalism is thus the source of its practical inferiority. To argue that society should be the controlled, programmed result of its members' activity is to demand that everyone should make their conduct functional to the overall social result in view. Thus, there can be no room for any form of conduct which, if generalised, would not lead to the programmed social outcome. Classical socialist doctrine finds it difficult to come to terms with political and social pluralism, understood not simply as a plurality of parties and trade unions but as the coexistence of various ways of working, producing and living, various and distinct cultural areas and levels of social existence.

So, too, with the commitment to equality, which has naturally nourished a centralist politics of collective provision and uniform administration. The modern administrative state has emerged out of this process, in which national provision has increasingly replaced local provision, voluntarism has been displaced by professionalization, and uniformity imposed on an untidy diversity. It need hardly be said that this process has brought with it many real achievements (though perhaps it does need to be said that bureaucracies do have considerable merits), but it has also involved a number of other consequences for socialism. It has been accompanied by the atrophy of the myriad forms of working-class self-help and democracy, as attention has become increasingly focused on the legislative possibilities of central state power. Thus A. H. Halsey describes the process whereby, in Britain, 'the Labour movement set out to nationalise democracy and welfare, to translate fraternity, equality and liberty from the local community to the national state' and in doing so was 'ironically fated to develop through its political party the threats of a bureaucratic state'. For these same reasons, a decentralist politics of territory tended to be subjugated to the centralizing politics of class.

From a number of directions, therefore, it is possible to chart the development of a socialist statism at the expense of alternative socialist traditions. However, in order to get these matters into clearer focus, it is necessary to say something about their place in traditional socialist thought. In some ways what is of most significance is how little space has in fact been occupied by serious discussion of structural and constitutional aspects of socialism, in terms of the organization of either a socialist economy or a socialist political system. Such preoccupations were part of the hallmark of the 'utopianism' from which Marx wanted to distance his own scientific socialism. It is well known that Marx was consistently dismissive of those who raised questions about the future organization of a socialist society, a futile pastime that was like writing 'recipes for the cookshops of the future'. The organization of future society would necessarily be a matter for those involved in making it.

THE MARXIAN VACUUM

This approach came to characterize the classical Marxist tradition. Thus Kautsky explained in *The Class Struggle* (1892) that concern with the structure of the future social order was 'wholly irreconcilable with the point of view of modern science', since it would be the determined product of the process of economic development that gave rise to it; so 'few things are, therefore, more childish than to demand of the socialist that he draw a picture of the commonwealth which he strives for'. If this seems sensible enough, consider also some of its assumptions and implications. It involves a refusal to think through the structural principles of socialist society, not merely its organizational details. The assumption is that there is only a single structural principle that matters, the replacement of private property by public property in the means of production, and that all else may be derived through practice from that.

This did not, of course, prevent Marx from describing the comprehensive transformation in the human condition that would flow from this single structural change. It inaugurated a realm of freedom, of unalienated creativity consequent upon the abolition of the division of labour, when it became possible for me to do one thing today and another tomorrow, to hunt in the morning, fish in the afternoon, rear cattle in the evening, criticise after dinner, just as I have a mind, without ever becoming hunter, fisherman, cowherd, or critic.

In citing this memorable formulation here the purpose is not to explore some of the familiar objections to it (for example, the technocratic objection – how does it apply to brain surgeons and airline pilots?) or the feminist objection (who does the cooking and washes the dishes?), but to identify a mode of thought in which it is possible to leap from an initial structural change to its most audacious consequences *with nothing else in between*. Indeed, attempts to clarify the character of this middle ground were likely to be dismissed as unscientific and unhistorical.

Thus, Marx offers an extended analysis of the political economy of capitalism but nothing similar for socialism. It is enough, it seems, that socialism is non-capitalism. In *Capital* there is reference to a socialist economy in terms of 'production by freely associated men . . . consciously regulated by them in accordance with a settled plan', but this is not thought to require any further consideration of the terms on which free association, conscious regulation, and settled plan might need to be reconciled as the basis for a workable, non-coercive socialist economy. It is not that Marx should have produced, in addition to his other prodigious labours, a working model of a socialist economy, but that his approach evidenced no recognition that a socialist economy would still be an arena of scarcity, choice, conflict, and decision. Such a recognition might seem important in itself, but it becomes even more important in view of the marked centralist bias in Marxist economic thought and its disparagement of the small-scale and particular. It is the centralizing, concentrationist thrust of capitalism that provides the necessary preconditions for socialism, replacing small production in industry and agriculture and needing only to be socialized to become the unitary economy of socialist rationality. As Kautsky once put it, socialist society was therefore to be seen as 'nothing more than a single gigantic industrial concern'.

In view of this, the question of how a wholly centralized socialist economy was to be run, and by whom, might seem to be of more than passing interest. In *The Economics of Feasible Socialism*, Alec Nove points attention (from his perspective as a leading authority on the old planned economies of Eastern Europe) to 'the fact that the functional logic of centralised planning "fits" far too easily into the practice of centralised despotism'. While there is no difficulty in showing that Marx was a radical democrat and republican apostle of liberty, it is also the case that he originated a mode of analysis which made it impossible to consider the problems raised by a possible 'fit' of this kind. It was the anarchist Bakunin who first pressed the question of how a centralized economy could be reconciled with political liberty, and it was a question to which Marx provided no adequate answer. Bakunin's own answer (which became the standard charge against Marxists from anarchists and syndicalists) was to point towards the creation of a new kind of state despotism by the 'scientific' socialists:

> The terms 'scientific socialist' and 'scientific socialism', which we meet incessantly in the works and speeches of the Lassallists and Marxists, are sufficient to prove that the so-called people's state will be nothing but a despotism over the masses, exercised by a new and quite small aristocracy of real or bogus 'scientists'. The people, being unlearned, will be completely exempted from the task of governing and will be forced into the herd of those who are governed. A fine sort of emancipation!

It is not enough, then, simply to acquit Marx of any despotic propensities, if at the same time it can be shown that his analysis left too many hostages to fortune. Bakunin's point is a real one, and it has gained added weight from the experience of post-revolutionary socialist societies in the twentieth century, in which the authority of Marxist 'science' has buttressed the power of ruling Marxist parties to produce the sort of despotic consequences with which the world has become all too familiar. It is scarcely adequate to claim that such consequences have nothing to do with classical Marxism (an inadequacy that does not, of course, prevent the claim being made) when it is evident that classical Marxism has refused to take seriously the whole question of socialist democracy, secure in the knowledge that the 'associated producers' will ensure that everything works out all right on the night. 'If Marxist political theory is to learn how to realise its own emancipatory project', writes John Dunn (in his *Western Political Theory in the Face of the Future*), 'it needs to develop a quite new level and style of reflection on the question of how in practice and in principle the battle of democracy could be won.'

This directs attention to Marxist political theory itself, the real centre of this whole discussion. Marx's inadequate treatment of the structural principles of socialism is a reflection of a theoretical position that deals inadequately with politics in general, reducing it to a subordinate and derivative status. There is no systematic political theorizing to be found in classical Marxism, for (as Miliband puts it in his *Marxism and Politics*) 'the available classical writings are simply silent or extremely perfunctory over major issues of politics and political theory'. Thus the absence of any sustained analysis of the state by Marx is matched by an equivalent neglect of the organizational problems of socialism. Those in search of Marx's understanding of the character of the provisional 'revolutionary dictatorship of the proletariat' or of the subsequent 'abolition of all classes' have to rummage amongst a scatter of often inconsistent references and usages. While this has provided much harmless diversion over the years for the scholarly army of Marx exegetes, it also emphasizes the gap where a coherent political analysis should be.

This gap was filled, at least with respect to political organization, only by Marx's assorted references to the necessity of a temporary (though also 'energetic') period of proletarian dictatorship, to be followed by a stateless communism in which 'there will be no more political power properly so-called'. The character of the revolutionary exercise of power by the proletariat as envisaged by Marx has always been a source of dispute. On the one hand, it is presented in terms of an intensification of centralized state power in the hands of the proletariat, as in his 1850 *March Address*, where Marx declared that 'the task of the really revolutionary party [is] to carry through the strictest centralisation'. On the other hand, though, in his discussion of the 1871 Paris Commune in *The Civil War in France*, Marx eulogized the decentralized democracy of the Commune that had been constructed on the smashed ruins of the existing state as 'the political form at last discovered under which to work out the economic emancipation of labour'. It represented Marx's belief that socialism would be distinguished, in David McLellan's phrase, by the 'deprofessionalisation of governmental functions'. Marx described what this meant in terms of the Commune:

> The majority of its members were naturally working men, or acknowl-edged representatives of the working class. The Commune was to be a working not a parliamentary body, executive and legislative at the same time. Instead of continuing to be the agent of the Central Government, the police was at once stripped of its political attributes, and turned into the responsible and at all times revocable agent of the Commune. So were the officials of all other branches of the Administration. From the members of the Commune downwards, the public service had to be done at workmen's wages. . . . Public functions ceased to be the private property of the tools of the Central Government. Not only municipal adminis-tration, but the whole initiative hitherto exercised by the state was laid into the hands of the Commune.

But did the Commune structure also represent, contrary to what Marx had seemed to suggest previously, the dictatorship of the proletariat (as Engels was later to declare), or was it to be seen as an anticipation of the durable political structure of a socialist society, even though the Commune itself was 'merely the rising of a city under exceptional circumstances' as Marx subsequently described it? What is significant is that this matter has to be left in the form of a question. Nowhere does Marx provide an answer to the key questions concerning the organization of the proletarian dictatorship, such as the terms on which central political power will connect with a decentralized commune structure and, in Bakunin's question, the sense in which the proletariat 'as a whole' would be in government.

LENIN AND THE END OF POLITICS

What is even more significant is that nowhere in classical Marxism is there a developed account of a socialist political system that confronts the basic questions to be asked of any political system. These are questions concerning the nature of representation and accountability, the organization of political competition and opposition, the methods by which conflicts are resolved, and the forms of political liberty. The reasons for this neglect are not difficult to locate. They spring from the derivative status of politics in the Marxist tradition, reflected in the belief that the state and the whole apparatus of 'bourgeois' political life was an expression of the class antagonism of capitalism and therefore destined to disappear when socialism abolished the cause of social antagonism. In Marx's words, 'there will be no more political power properly so-called'. A unitary society, without classes, would not require the political machinery needed by a divided society. In practice, of course, this was to be converted into the rule of the single party in the name of the single class, sustained by the definitional denial that any grounds for political division and opposition could exist. Nor can this be dismissed as an illegitimate conversion, when it derives from a theoretical tradition that identifies political (and other) antagonisms as essentially a derivation from class antagonisms. The twentieth-century party-state has finally buried this model of political dependency (or should have done), even though it is itself constructed out of the theoretical tradition that produced it. The lesson of its demise merely confirmed this lesson of its life.

It is not sufficient, therefore, to register the fact that the classical Marxist tradition neglects to offer a developed account of the organizational structure of socialism, unless it is also understood that such neglect is not an oversight but an authentic expression of its central assumptions. The only structural change that mattered was in property relations, from which all else would flow, in ways that could not be anticipated by utopian speculation but would be determined by the historical actors themselves. However, socialism's abolition of the class antagonism that sustained the political machinery of capitalism was the guarantee of an integrated democracy under socialism, the reflection of a unitary society. There could be no more comprehensive guarantee than this, requiring no elaborate small print. It promised, quite literally, an end to politics. Some kind of 'public power' would remain, but there was no need to quibble about the simple administrative forms that this would take.

The promise was fulfilled, though scarcely in the form intended. Those regimes that transmuted this mode of thought into their official ideology did indeed deliver an end to politics, or at least the closest approximation to it that the world has yet seen. The crucial, poignant, figure in this process is Lenin. It was Lenin who, in his *State and Revolution*, written on the eve of the Bolshevik revolution, translated the general conception of an end to politics into an account of the structure of popular self-administration that would replace the state in post-revolutionary society. It was also Lenin who, in the wake of the revolution, presided over the development of an authoritarianism rooted in the 'democratic centralism' of a single party and a repressive state bureaucracy. There is no need to resort to a cynical explanation to account for this shift. The former represented Lenin's solution in terms of Marxist *theory* to the question of post-revolutionary organization, while the latter represented his solution in *practice*. Only those attached to a particular view of the unity of theory and practice need be surprised by such a disjuncture.

Something was said earlier about Lenin's need, contrary to the familiar view of him as a revolutionary opportunist, to ground his political practice in a secure basis of Marxist theory. If this was true of his account of the conditions which made revolution possible, it was also true of his account of post-revolutionary society. He satisfied himself, following Bukharin, that a Marxist revolution would need to destroy the existing state machine and, following Marx, that it would be replaced by a system of popular self-government on the Commune model. Thus it was Lenin, in his *State and Revolution*, who (as Harding puts it) 'rescued the commune from oblivion'. He argued that Marx's description of the Commune had established the correct form of socialist organization; that the soviets were the practical embodiment of this form; and that capitalist imperialism had developed the processes of production and distribution to an organizational point at which they could be run on simplified lines by a system of popular self-administration.

What this would mean was confidently described by Lenin in this familiar passage:

> We the workers, shall organize large-scale production on the basis of what capitalism has already created, relying on our own experience as workers, establishing strict, iron discipline backed up by the state power of the armed workers. We shall reduce the role of state officials to that of simply carrying out our instructions as responsible, revocable, modestly paid 'foremen and accountants'. . . . This is our proletarian task, this is what

we can and must start with in accomplishing the proletarian revolution. Such a beginning, on the basis of large-scale production, will of itself lead to the gradual 'withering away' of all bureaucracy, to the gradual creation of an order ... under which the functions of control and accounting, becoming more and more simple, will be performed by each in turn, will then become a habit and will finally die out as the special functions of a special section of the population.

This account of a decentralized, participatory democracy under socialism (in which 'all will govern in turn and will soon become accustomed to no one governing') represents the culmination of a tradition. It is the fulfilment of Marx's original Promethean, emancipatory vision of active self-government, the final realization of the classical democratic ideal itself.

However, as the culmination of a tradition it is also the place (as A. J. Polan has argued to such good effect in his *Lenin and the End of Politics*) where the flaws in that tradition stand out in sharpest relief. There is the underlying assumption that political and administrative consequences can simply be read off from an analysis of economic development. There is the repudiation of 'bourgeois' politics that takes literally the idea that, under socialism, the government of men is replaced by the administration of things. There is the assumption that the social unity represented by socialism means that there can be no legitimate grounds for organized disunity. Thus Lenin reflects a tradition that offers democracy without division, administration without politics, civic activity without civil liberty. Behind the lyrical account of a self-managing society, there lurks the 'state power of the armed workers', while the absence of any discussion of the party in *State and Revolution* (confined to a single, fleeting reference) simply served to identify the political vacuum that it was destined to fill. Lenin's earlier *What is to be Done?* was to prove a more reliable guide to the organizational imperatives of socialist revolution.

It is difficult to overstate the significance of Leninism, in this respect as in others, and of what may be called the Leninist moment in the development of socialist forms. Established positions and traditional assumptions were thrown into confusion.

Classical Marxism, certainly as represented by the Second International theorists, had assumed that socialism would extend existing democratic forms, not negate them. Thus Kautsky was quick to denounce the political despotism of Bolshevism, but this denunciation also served to expose how unexplored had been the political assumptions of the whole Marxist tradition. Perhaps the most telling critique of Bolshevik political repression from within the Marxist tradition came from Rosa Luxemburg, not on the sort of general liberal grounds advanced by Kautsky but on the grounds that political dictatorship by the party prevented the free development of the class. The revolution required political freedom and democracy if it was not to atrophy: 'Without general elections, without unrestricted freedom of press and assembly, without a free struggle of opinion, life dies out in every public institution, becomes a mere semblance of life, in which only the bureaucracy remains as the active element.' However, Luxemburg's point could be put rather differently: Bolshevism had demonstrated that it was an illusion to suppose that socialist revolution would necessarily take a democratic, libertarian form and that despotic, bureaucratic forms were also available (and, perhaps, more likely).

Such matters did not present themselves so clearly to most socialists in the immediate aftermath of the Bolshevik revolution, or in the turbulent period that followed the end of the First World War. It was possible to regard the soviets as the concrete form of direct democracy under socialism, the solution in socialist terms to the question of political organization. Thus, in Italy in 1918–20 Gramsci could present the Turin workers' council movement as part of this same 'council' conception of socialist democracy, in opposition to rule by party, parliament, or bureaucracy. It was a form of power that came from below, not imposed from the top, and the organizational structure of socialist society was to be seen in terms of a network of relationships between working-class institutions:

> To link these institutions, coordinating and ordering them into a highly centralised hierarchy of competencies and powers, while respecting the necessary autonomy and articulation of each, is to create a genuine workers' democracy here and now – a workers' democracy in effective and active opposition to the bourgeois State, and prepared to replace it here and now in all its essential functions of administering and controlling the national heritage.

This 'conciliar' communism was destined to become a minority tradition following the collapse of the postwar working-class militancy (its continued advocacy in the interwar years being associated with such forgotten figures as the Dutch anti-Bolshevik Pannekoek). Much of it was simply swallowed up in Lenin's organization of an international communism to wrest the leadership of the western working class from reformist social democracy. Even those who, in significant senses, were not Leninists were forced in this polarization to range themselves on the side of 'revolution' against 'reform'. This involved, as with Gramsci, a shift of emphasis from council to party as the organizational model. It also involved a belief on the part of many anti-authoritarian revolutionaries that 'after the revolution', or more accurately after the period of discipline and dictatorship necessary to consolidate the revolution, then the way would be clear for the establishment of a self-governing society of the kind outlined in Lenin's *State and Revolution*. For example, the syndicalist Tom Mann could declare that 'the outlook for the future is not that of a centralised official bureaucracy giving instructions and commands to servile subordinates (but) . . . the coming of associations of equals'; but could then go on to affirm his support for the Third International because 'with the experience of Russia to guide us, I entirely agree that there will be a period, short or long, when the dictatorship of the proletariat must be resorted to'. Even at the time this was written, the soviets were already being subsumed by party and state. Soon there would be everything from 'Soviet' power to 'Soviet' circuses; but the only thing there would not be were the soviets.

COLLECTIVISM AND ITS CRITICS

If the organized split within international socialism had the effect, reinforced by the slackening of the postwar working-class militancy, that by the early 1920s the libertarian and self-managing strands of Marxism had been effectively buried by an authoritarian communism, then a similar process had occurred on the other side of the socialist divide. In Britain, for example, the Fabians had developed a collectivist doctrine that represented the quintessential administrative version of socialism. In his contribution to *Fabian Essays*, Bernard Shaw explained 'the distinctive term Social Democrat' as

> indicating the man or woman who desires through Democracy to gather the whole people into the State, so that the State may be trusted with the rent of the country, and finally with the land, the capital, and the organisation of the national industry – with all the sources of production, in short, which are now abandoned to the cupidity of irresponsible private individuals.

It should, perhaps, be said that the early Fabians were not quite the rigid state centralists they are often described as, not least because of the municipal emphasis that envisaged a major role for the local state. Nor should the historical reputation of Fabianism be allowed to obscure the fact that other strands in early British socialism were associational rather than organizational, as reflected in Keir Hardie's ethical socialism that expected a period of statism to be merely the necessary preliminary to a mutualist communism or, more significantly, in William Morris's powerful rejection of state socialism in both its revolutionary and reformist versions and consistent advocacy of an associational socialism of decentralized self-government.

However, when these qualifications are entered, it remains the case that classical Fabianism represented a particular kind of socialism. It was a collectivist kind that emphasized the organizational attributes of socialism in arranging efficient production and egalitarian distribution through its control of the national and local state. It also set its face against other kinds of socialism – not merely against revolutionary socialism, but against all those kinds of socialism in which self-government (usually of producers) was the central emphasis. This gives a particular interest to the period, roughly the second decade of the twentieth century, when Fabian collectivism was challenged by the ideas of the guild socialists (at a time when industrial militancy had raised demands for workers' control, and when the sovereignty of the state was under intellectual challenge from the pluralists). The guild socialists, with G. D. H. Cole as their leading figure, argued that socialism was about freedom and self-government, crucially in the workplace but extending throughout society; and looked forward to the development of the trade unions from their present negative, defensive role into self-governing industrial guilds responsible for the control of industry and forming the nucleus of a guild society.

Guild socialism claimed to be a synthesis of syndicalism and collectivism. The former was right in its emphasis on the centrality of industrial freedom, but was flawed by a sectionalism that failed to acknowledge a general interest that included the interests of consumers. The latter avoided the central defect of syndicalism but also its crucial merit. The elaborate system building of the guild socialists was designed to construct a workable synthesis between these positions. If the infirmities and dangers of collectivism were particularly emphasized, it was because they represented a future that was already immanent in the present. In his *Self-Government in Industry* (1917), Cole noted how 'today we are moving at a headlong pace in the direction of a "national" control of the lives of men'; and how 'in the State of today, in which democratic control through Parliament is little better than a farce, the Collectivist State would be the Earthly Paradise of bureaucracy'. It might offer more security, but it would not change the subordinate status of the workers nor offer more general scope for the exercise of freedom and democracy. Because of this, it would not effect any significant change in human motivation, and would not prove to be a kind of socialism capable of producing a popular response on a durable basis. Imposed from the top, it would wither from below.

Like the 'council' movement within Marxism, guild socialism was destined to fade from view in the early 1920s, another victim of the great socialist divide. Yet for a time it had seemed that guild socialist and associated ideas had opened up an alternative direction for socialism in Britain. There had taken place a period of sustained debate, for over a decade, on the structural form of socialism, combining political theory and practical example. This debate had addressed such key issues as the balance between producer and consumer interests, democracy and efficiency, territorial and functional devolution. In 1920 both Cole (in his *Guild Socialism Restated*) and the Webbs (in their *Constitution for the Socialist Commonwealth of Great Britain*) offered their developed thoughts on the structural form of socialism. If their emphasis remained different, both positions reflected a prevailing belief that it was important to think through the structural form of the distribution of power under socialism (and that such matters could not simply be left until, and be resolved by, the coming of socialism). The socialist basis adopted by the Labour Party in 1918, with its coupling of 'common ownership' and 'popular administration', reflected this prevailing climate of ideas.

Yet this opening towards a decentralized, self-managing version of socialism was to be effectively sealed off for the next half-century. It found no place in the organized antagonism between communists and social democrats. The former had adopted a model of party authoritarianism while the latter had settled for a cautious reformism that involved protestations of faith in existing constitutional arrangements. Economic depression took its toll of the labour movement's energy and imagination and turned eyes towards the state as the means of redress. The widespread attraction of the idea of economic planning (influenced by the Russian example) served to strengthen the emphasis on state centralism, while the opportunities opened up by Keynesian ideas of demand management pushed more gently in the same direction. The dark shadows cast by fascism and Stalinism could be interpreted in terms of the need to be wary of new political forms and to settle for established ones. This is historical shorthand, of course, but the effects of these assorted influences were evident in a political practice that was increasingly deaf to the distant voices of a socialist pluralism. In Britain, for example, socialization became nationalization and in the bureaucratic form of the public corporation that denied the claims of producer or consumer democracy; while the 1945 Labour Government can now be seen to have been 'sternly centralist' (K. O. Morgan, *Labour in Power 1945–1951*), despite the former guild socialist sympathies of its prime minister.

In one significant respect, however, this story can be told less negatively. The political experiences of the twentieth century at least provided the materials out of which could be constructed a 'democratic socialism' with an identity sharply different from its authoritarian form (although the fact that so many socialists in the West fudged this task for so long is also part of the history of our times). No longer could it be supposed that the conversion of private into public ownership of the means of production was sufficient to make redundant any concern with the political organization of freedom. R. H. Tawney, as ever, made the essential point:

> The truth is that a conception of Socialism which views it as involving the nationalization of everything except political power, on which all else depends, is not, to speak with moderation, according to light. The question is not merely whether the State owns and controls the means of production. It is also who owns and controls the State.

Moreover, this question could be regarded as more, not less, important for socialists to tackle in so far as socialism would augment the general power of the state by adding economic power to political power. This last point had been emphasized earlier by Jaurès, when he presented socialism (in his *Socialist Organisation*) in terms of a diversification of economic power and decentralization of political power:

> If the politicians and administrators who already control the nation's diplomacy and armed forces were also given authority over the whole labour force, and if they could appoint managers at all levels in the same way as they now appoint army officers, this would confer on a handful of men such power as Asian despots never dreamt of – for they controlled only the surface of public life and not the economy of their countries.

It became important, therefore, for democratic socialists to identify their kind of socialism as involving civil and political liberty and effective mechanisms for political representation and accountability, as well as delineating the respective roles of the market and the state. It would incorporate and extend the democratic freedoms won under capitalism, not abrogate them in the name of an illusory conception of 'socialist' freedom.

However, the construction of a democratic socialist position of this kind confronted a number of difficulties. It was undermined by a communist version of Marxism which propagated the view, most successfully in the 'red decade' of the 1930s, that the whole apparatus of 'capitalist' freedom and democracy was essentially bogus because of its class character. However, it also faced dilution from a version of social democracy that responded to its loss of theoretical and political confidence by slackening its attachment to socialism in its blanket embrace of existing constitutional and institutional arrangements. The twentieth century had made it harder, if more necessary, to link socialism and democracy; and harder still to argue for a democratic socialism that did not merely affirm the compatability of socialism and parliamentary democracy but went beyond this to offer a kind of socialism which had democracy as its active, organizing principle.

AN ENABLING SOCIALISM?

But was there, and is there, an available democratic socialism of this kind? Or is it the case, as critics of socialism have long argued, that the organizational imperatives of socialism can lead only (at best) to bureaucratic rule and (at worst) to something even more tyrannical? 'I for one cannot visualise', wrote Schumpeter, 'in the conditions of modern society, a socialist organization in any form other than that of a huge and all embracing bureaucratic apparatus.' Such questions could, perhaps, be avoided by socialists for as long as they remained at the level of theory; but during the course of the twentieth century they became urgent questions from the world of political practice. Even where a self-managing socialism had been established, as in the old Yugoslavia, the maintenance of the dominant political role of the party prevented it being taken as evidence of the combination of socialism and democracy. The abundant evidence that it was quite possible for them not to be combined, and the lack of evidence of a more positive kind, came to have a profound influence on socialist thinking (and on thinking about socialism). In the 1940s, reviewing Hayek's *The Road to Serfdom*, George Orwell summed up 'our present predicament' in these terms:

> Capitalism leads to dole queues, the scramble for markets, and war. Collectivism leads to concentration camps, leader worship and war. There is no way out of this unless a planned economy can somehow be combined with the freedom of the intellect.

Orwell went on to register the depressing fact that nobody seemed able to translate this 'somehow' into a practical programme. If this sounded like the voice of the mid-century reaction to Stalinism, the democratic socialist predicament could still be expressed in remarkably similar terms two decades later. In *The Long Revolution*, Raymond Williams described the deadlock in thinking about social change that stemmed from the fact that

> we seem reduced to a choice between speculator and bureaucrat, and while we do not like the speculators, the bureaucrat is not exactly inviting either. In such a situation, energy is sapped, hope weakens, and of course the present compromise between the speculators and the bureaucrats remains unchallenged.

An authoritarian model of socialism was on offer from the communists, while social democratic collectivism seemed able only to offer the prospect of an enlarged state bureaucracy as the organizational model of a welfare capitalism. If this prospect caused some socialist voices to be raised in resistance (for example, in the postwar *New Fabian Essays* Richard

Crossman argued that 'the planned economy and the centralisation of power are no longer socialist objectives'), for a long time these remained minority voices and their effect was to reinforce the retreat from socialism rather than to promote its democratic restatement.

However, in this respect as in others, the loosening of the rival socialist blocs in the 1950s and 1960s served to produce its consequences. An independent Marxism could begin to undertake its own critique of the Soviet state, turning from Leninism to Gramsci and reclaiming a tradition of 'council' communism, and endeavouring to restate the emancipatory promise of original Marxism in terms capable of carrying at least some conviction in the late-twentieth-century world. The cultural revolution in the West in the 1960s found its political expression (most conspicuously in the *événements* of 1968) in a rejection of the bureaucratic character of both organized communism and organized social democracy, and in a reassertion of libertarian and self-managing traditions (not always, it might be added, in very libertarian ways). A central aspect of Eurocommunism also involved the acknowledgement of the validity of the western model of political democracy; while in the socialist parties of Europe there developed a renewed interest in producer democracy and the democratic diffusion of power. In France, for example, 'autogestion' was a key ideological element in the revival of French socialism in the 1970s. During the same period Swedish socialism (partly in response to the offensive from radical liberalism) reformulated its doctrinal basis to emphasize the role of producer democracy in the general extension of democracy that was now identified as the distinctive project of democratic socialism. In Germany, too, part of the process of reversing the deradicalization of German socialism that had culminated in the 1959 Bad Godesberg programme turned on the need for a democratic, non-bureaucratic socialism in which 'basis groups' would share power with the state. The Bad Godesberg programme had contained the famous formulation 'competition as far as possible, planning as far as necessary'. In 1974 this could be nicely reformulated (by the left-wing Social Democrat Strasser): 'As much autogestion as possible, as much central planning and administration as necessary.'

More generally, some of the most innovative socialist thought in Europe during this period (for example, the work of Gorz and Bahro) was concerned to argue the case for the contemporary relevance of an autonomist, decentralized version of socialism and the irrelevance of organizational, productionist versions. The technological arguments that were formerly deployed against a small-scale, self-managing socialism could now be stood on their head. From within the communist world itself, dissident and reformist voices explored new pluralist possibilities in relation both to the economy and to the polity. For a time it even began to seem plausible that a social democracy that was moving in a more radical direction might connect with a communism that was reforming itself to produce quite new organizational models.

In fact, this turned out to be the briefest of interludes. Far from becoming bolder, social democracy was driven further back by the unexpectedly rampant revival of market liberalism, while the collapse of communism did not bring with it any desire to explore any other forms of socialism on the part of those who had just managed to emancipate themselves from one version. If the 1970s had seemed to open up new thinking on the structural forms of socialism, by the 1990s it seemed to be much more a case of clinging desperately to the battered wreckage of old thinking.

It seems reasonably clear that a democratic socialism seriously committed to *both* socialism *and* democracy and seeking to present socialism in essentially democratic terms would need to have theorized a structure that would make this possible. In political terms, this would require an attention to the constitutional structure of a socialist society, in which the state would continue to exist as the major focus for collective decisions but would need to be securely rooted in a developed and decentralized structure of political representation, political pluralism, and political and civic freedom. In other words, a political structure in which there was more democracy, not less. In economic terms, it would require (as Alec Nove has argued in *The Economics of Feasible Socialism*) an economic structure in which social ownership took a diversity of forms, there was a preference for the small-scale and the self-managing, central economic planning was confined to major strategic decisions, market choice and competition operated subject to certain ground rules, and some material inequality was accepted as necessary for a free labour market but was consciously limited. In other words, an economic structure in which there was plan and market, centralism and decentralization, state control and self-management. A democratic socialism of this kind would be one in which democracy did not stop at the factory gate, nor at the factory exit. It would be an empowering and an enabling socialism, both politically and economically. However, it would also be a kind of socialism which has been a minority tradition for much of socialism's history.

6   Actors

> The crisis of socialism is above all a reflection of the crisis of the proletariat.
>
> André Gorz

If socialism is to come, who is to bring it about? Who are its actors and agents? In terms of the general line of argument being pursued here, such familiar questions require a further refinement: what kinds of actors are envisaged and embraced by what kinds of socialism? For a long time it seemed that socialists had a secure, unproblematical answer to this central question of agency, with any difficulties confined to the margin. At the end of the twentieth century this is manifestly no longer the case. If it has become possible for a socialist like André Gorz to wave a convincing *Farewell to the Working Class*, it is much less clear to whom socialists are now waving a convincing greeting.

THE AGENTS OF SOCIALISM

Why has this matter of agency moved to the centre of socialist discussion? Why has an old axiom (the working class as the carrier of socialism) turned into a new question? A number of issues are clearly involved here, but perhaps two in particular should be identified at once because of their central importance. At this stage they are only sketched out, to be returned to later. Firstly, there is the extent to which, in socialist political practice, the movement of a class has been converted into the organization of a party. The working class as socialist actor has been supplemented by the party as the agent of the class. At one level, this may be said merely to have raised necessary questions about the relationship of class to party. At another level, however, it has opened up the whole question of 'substitutism', the extent to which the party has not just supplemented class action but substituted itself for it. Moreover, as Trotsky had warned in 1904, this process could be carried further: 'the party organisation at first substitutes itself for the party as a whole; then the central committee substitutes itself for the organisation; and finally a single "dictator" substitutes himself for the central committee.' For obvious reasons, this process of substitution has been seen as having a particular application to the twentieth-century communist tradition. However, it should also be noted that similar lines of analysis have been pursued in relation to the social democratic parties.

The second main reason for the contemporary preoccupation with the matter of socialist agency may be stated even more bluntly. Socialism's traditional actors have not displayed a reliable talent for keeping to their script. Not only do they frequently get their lines wrong, but they sometimes even seem to think they are taking part in a different production. The western working class has not merely failed to fulfil the revolutionary role assigned to it by classical Marxism (a role last glimpsed in the second decade of this century), but has seemed to become ever *less* revolutionary. Lenin's fears after 1914 that the western working class, unless given decisive revolutionary leadership, would be incorporated into 'bourgeois reformism' through the treacherous agency of the social democrats would seem to have been amply vindicated. However, even in reformist terms, working-class support for social democracy has not generally been sufficient to secure the durable reconstruction of these societies on a social democratic basis. The experience of fascism (an experience that included the fact that over 30 per cent of Nazi Party members were manual workers, part of a class that had been regarded as the most promising socialist material in Europe) opened up the prospect of a mass mobilization of the Right and dented (in some cases, even inverted) traditional socialist expectations. In recent decades the changing character of class structures in the West has been identified as presenting new questions concerning the political role of the working class, and of socialist agency in general; while outside the West such questions have been asked and answered in ways that have introduced socialist actors of new kinds in unfamiliar roles.

Against this sort of background, it is scarcely surprising then that the matter of socialist agency has acquired considerable significance today. In the 1840s Marx dismissed and derided the 'utopian' socialists on the same grounds. The absence of any convincing agency in their schemes was a reflection of the unhistorical and unscientific character of their general approach, and constituted the basis of their utopianism. Thus Saint-Simon presented his 'system' to successive regimes in France and in particular to a motley assortment of groups (*les industriels*) who would reorganize society on a new productionist basis; meanwhile Fourier sat around waiting for the patron who would fund the social experiments that would vindicate his schemes and save the world from its misery. It was against such utopianism that the young Marx directed his materialist account of the motor of historical development. As the famous opening words of the *Communist Manifesto* announced it, 'The history of all hitherto existing society is the history of class struggles'.

When translated into the present, what this meant was that socialists did not have to cast around for a suitable agency for the socialist project but merely to recognize that both the project and its agent were immanent in the historical process itself. What was required was an initial act of recognition, not of invention. Capitalism was the contemporary form of the class appropriation of the means of production but, like previous appropriations, it had generated its own internal forces of antagonism and eventual transcendence. These forces were represented by the proletariat, the creation of capitalism but also its antagonist and revolutionary successor. The proletariat would develop in size, strength, organization and consciousness as capitalism itself developed. In this process it would develop from a class *in* itself to a class *for* itself. A progressive simplification of class forces was underway, as intermediate, petty-bourgeois elements were swallowed up by the class polarization into the 'two great hostile camps' of bourgeoisie and proletariat. The hostility would reach its 'decisive hour' in conditions of capitalist crisis and proletarian pauperization, when the proletariat would emancipate itself through a revolution of the 'immense majority' and thereby also deliver humanity from the final form of class oppression and antagonism. 'What the bourgeoisie therefore, produces, above all, is its own gravediggers. Its fall and the victory of the proletariat are equally inevitable.'

So here was the installation of the working class as the revolutionary subject, the carrier of socialism. If the sketch given here is in the dramatic idiom of the *Manifesto*, needing to be filled out and qualified in various respects to take account of later positions, it does nevertheless represent the essential Marxist perspective. Socialism was to be achieved through the revolutionary action of the working class; indeed, socialism *was* the revolutionary victory of the working class. There could be no question of whether class struggle was desirable or undesirable, since it was the essential fact about social and economic life under capitalism. It conditioned everything else, and was destined to end in a particular kind of resolution. It was reflected in the various forms of struggle of labour against capital, and in the developing industrial and political organization of the forces of labour. There might be room for argument and adjustment about the precise moment and conditions in which the proletariat would come to power, but that it would come to power was as certain as that night followed day. It did not matter either that Marx had offered no sustained account of the nature of social class, since classes defined themselves in terms of their relationship to the means of production and revealed themselves through action.

Before turning to some of the issues that have been associated with this identification of the revolutionary subject by Marx, something should be said about the nature of the identification itself. It is an indication of the severity of the contemporary crisis in socialist thought on the matter of agency that, even from within the Marxist tradition, voices have come to be heard asking not only the now familiar questions about the relationship between class position and class behaviour but, beyond this, the fundamental question concerning the identification of the revolutionary subject itself. Put simply, what if Marx got it wrong? This question has been framed not just in terms of the evident gap between the prospectus and the performance, but in terms that cast doubt on the basis of the original identification. As Rudolf Bahro has written, 'It might well have been no more than a Hegelian error to have burdened a particular class, and a class restricted by its position in the reproduction process, with the fate of humanity as a whole'.

In other words, the world-historic mission of the proletariat begins to look like a philosophical invention on Marx's part. It was the product of a position that held that – to paraphrase the words of *The Holy Family* quoted earlier – what mattered was what the proletariat essentially *was* and, because of what it was, what it would necessarily *do*. Its historical role was assigned to it without an audition. Nor did it matter that its performance in the leading historical role might cast doubt on its ability as an actor, or might even suggest that it was unaware of what its role actually was, since it would necessarily 'become what it is'. For Marx, then, it was not observation of the proletariat in action that provided the basis for his casting (nor his own limited engagement with working-class political activity), but initially and primarily it was the product of a process of philosophical reflection. This extended into, and was sustained by, a view of capitalist development as involving a homogenizing proletarianization of labour carried to a point at which a class of collective labourers having nothing to lose but their chains has both the capacity and the necessity to free itself through an act of collective appropriation. However, this account of proletarianization was again not the product of historical analysis but a working out of what the proletariat would have to become and do because of what, in *essence*, it was. This point is well made by Gorz:

> Marx described the process of proletarianisation in such a way as to show that it would produce a proletariat conscious of its being, that is to say, forced by vital necessity to become what it is to be. The historical analysis was so weak, however, that it was incapable of factually supporting the thesis it was designed to underpin. At his conclusion, Marx had returned to his point of departure and had failed to develop an analysis which substantially enriched his initial intuition.

It would, of course, be absurd to conclude from this that socialism had acquired an agency simply through a process of philosophical invention on Marx's part. It was plausible to believe that the class of wage labourers that had been brought into existence by capitalism, and that was the victim of the systematic exploitation revealed by Marx's analysis of the operation of the capitalist economy, would also be the class that would provide the opposition to capitalism. It was this class, the working class, that had a direct *interest* in opposing capitalism. This interest was reflected in the development of industrial and political organizations of the working class. In terms of numbers and organization, the nineteenth-century working class could plausibly be regarded as the *rising* class. Thus, Marx's nomination of the proletariat as the socialist actor was not an eccentric nomination, even if it was the product of philosophical deduction rather than empirical observation.

CLASS AND PARTY

The point is, though, that Marx had not merely found an actor but had also written a script. The historical role of the proletariat was to overthrow capitalism and establish socialism. It would develop both the ability and the necessity to accomplish this. In performing this role it was acting not merely on behalf of itself but on behalf of the whole of humanity, and was therefore to be regarded as the universal class. It was in this form that the proletariat as socialist actor entered Marxist politics. Its entry in this form carried with it a number of significant consequences for socialist thinking. One such consequence was the socialist belief that the existence of a revolutionary proletariat was not the guarantee of socialism, but rather that the necessity of socialism was the guarantee of a revolutionary proletariat. This belief sustained Marxists as they waited for the proletariat to become what it was, and enabled them to explain away the frequent postponement of capitalism's final crisis in the knowledge that next time (or the next) it would be different. When the western working class behaved in ways that it should not have done (as in 1914), this could be blamed on the treachery of its leadership. When capitalist democracy was challenged by a mass movement (as it was in the 1930s by fascism), this could be interpreted as marking the last stage of capitalism's crisis and therefore the prelude to socialism, even though to the untutored eye it might suggest the possibility of a movement-regime of a rather different kind.

Even though the proletariat might not look like a revolutionary class, the fact that it *was* constituted its special status. In so far as it carried the entire human project upon its own shoulders, no sacrifice was too great in its service. In the case of the syndicalist Sorel, attachment to the 'heroic' role of the proletariat as militant, historical actor even supplanted its role as the agent of socialism. Syndicalism in general, of course, looked to the industrial workers as the direct, unmediated actors of socialism, challenging capitalism at the point of production rather than through the circuitous, misleading channels of parties and parliaments. This was associated with a badge of authenticity in the form of an exclusive proletarianism: *'Pas de mains blanches, mais seulement les mains calleuses!'* If it was asked how the proletariat was to develop from a class in itself to a class for itself, syndicalists would point to the class development occasioned by the general strike. Lenin, too, despite his emphasis on leadership and organization, explained how revolutionary situations overturned routine assumptions and served as a school of political education for the class of socialist actors: 'During a revolution millions and tens of millions of people learn in a week more than they do in a year of ordinary, somnolent life.'

Lenin's remark pointed to an important shift of emphasis. The proletariat would learn to play its revolutionary role *during* a revolutionary upheaval, not as a necessary prelude to such an upheaval. In other words, the proletariat retained its role as socialist actor but its ability to perform this role, even its consciousness that this *was* its role, now depended upon the ability of other actors to promote the conditions in which this class development would take place. This shift of emphasis, about which more will need to be said in a moment, directs attention to a permanent tension within the Marxist tradition on the question of socialist actors. Its origin is to be found in the need to reconcile the (philosophically) necessary role of the proletariat as socialist actor with its (actual) capacity and consciousness to perform this role. Marx described the process whereby this happy reconciliation would be brought about through the character of capitalist development itself. However, even in Marx's own writings there remains the uneasy coexistence of a proletariat enslaved by the ideological hegemony of capitalism and a proletariat expected to act as the revolutionary agent of its own emancipation. This indicated a problem, even though its existence was neither acknowledged nor explored. However, it remained as a characteristic tension within the Marxist tradition. The tension is that between the proletariat as the false-conscious dupes of capitalism and the (same) proletariat as the self-conscious creators of the new society and the new humanity.

If this tension is most evident with Lenin, it is also Lenin who confronts the problem at its source most directly. The problem is that of the relationship between proletariat, labour movement, and socialism. The working class created a working-class movement, but was there a necessary connection between the working-class movement and socialism? Such troubling questions remained hidden beneath the surface of Marx's account of the organic evolution of a class towards organization and consciousness, an account that sustained the outlook of Second International orthodoxy. It is true that Marx identified the special role of the 'communists' in providing practical and theoretical service to the working-class movement in the process whereby the proletariat developed into a revolutionary class. Their political role had its basis in the fact that (as the *Manifesto* put it) 'in the realm of theory they have over the great mass of the proletariat the advantage of clearly understanding the line of march, the conditions, and the ultimate general results of the proletarian movement'. Their special status as the most advanced section of the working-class movement derived from their superior understanding of what the proletariat essentially *was*, in terms of its larger purposes and revolutionary destiny. However, they formed no separate party of their own and 'have no interests separate and apart from those of the proletariat as a whole'.

If this might appear to raise problems concerning the role of the proletariat as socialist actor, it was not allowed to. Even if it seemed that the role of the proletariat would be acted out only with the support of other actors able to prompt from the wings on the basis of their superior knowledge of the script, the relationship between these sets of actors was treated as unproblematical. For this reason Marx nowhere offers an extended account of the relationship between the proletariat and its 'advanced' section, or of the general relationship between class and party. The problem is defined out of existence by the organic, developmental way in which it makes its appearance. This unproblematical treatment is also to be found in the orthodoxies of the Second International period. It is acknowledged that the working class needs to be serviced by socialist theorists on its path to consciousness and power, but this servicing operation is treated as a natural part of an organic process of class development and is not regarded as raising any particular difficulties of its own.

All this needs to be recorded, since Lenin is frequently presented as having broken with orthodoxy in his discussion of these matters. In important respects, Lenin was able to echo Social Democratic orthodoxy in his treatment of class, party and consciousness. Thus, in *What is to be Done?* he is able to cite the authority of Karl Kautsky for the latter's 'profoundly true' remarks on the relationship between socialism and the working class. As Kautsky wrote (and was quoted by Lenin):

> Socialist consciousness is represented as a necessary and direct result of the proletarian class struggle. But this is absolutely untrue. . . . Socialism and the class struggle arise side by side and not one out of the other; each arises under different conditions. Modern socialist consciousness can arise only on the basis of profound scientific knowledge. . . . The

vehicle of science is not the.proletariat, but the bourgeois intelligentsia: it was in the minds of individual members of this stratum that modern socialism originated, and it was they who communicated it to the more intellectually developed proletarians who, in their turn, introduce it into the proletarian class struggle where conditions allow that to be done. Thus, socialist consciousness is something introduced into the proletarian class struggle from without, and not something that arises within it spontaneously.

Because this sounds like the authentic voice of Leninism it needs to be recorded that it is also the authoritative voice of Social Democratic orthodoxy. Moreover, it was an analysis that implied a key role for the Social Democratic party in equipping the revolutionary actor with its appropriate theoretical equipment. In Kautsky's definition, the party was the 'confluence of socialism and the working class'.

It is clear, then, that Lenin did not break new ground in arguing that class position was not a spontaneous generator of socialist consciousness, and that for such generation to occur a party and a vanguard must actively intervene. It is also the case that Lenin emphasized the need for the vanguard party to maintain close links with the workers and their struggles, an expression of the essential unity of theory and practice. Nor was it remarkable or shocking that Lenin should point out that Marx and Engels were members of the bourgeois intelligentsia, or that socialist theory generally was to be expected to emanate from this same source. Why then does Leninism nevertheless have to be regarded as an important moment in the development of socialist thinking on actors and agents, and in particular on the relationship between party and class?

The answer is not to be found in this oft-quoted passage from *What is to be Done?* on the matter of working-class consciousness:

We have said that there could not have been social-democratic consciousness among the workers. It would have had to be brought to them from without. The history of all countries shows that the working class, exclusively by its own effort, is able to develop only trade union consciousness.

As has been seen, the Leninist innovation does not turn on this matter of consciousness 'from without', which was already part of a prevailing orthodoxy. What it does turn on, however, is revealed by a further passage from the same text:

Since there can be no question of an independent ideology formulated by the working masses themselves in the process of their movement, the only choice is – either bourgeois or socialist ideology. There is no middle course (for mankind has not created a 'third' ideology, and in a society torn by class antagonisms there can never be a non-class or an above-class ideology). . . . There is much talk of spontaneity. But the spontaneous development of the working-class movement leads to its subordination to bourgeois ideology . . . for the spontaneous working-class movement is trade-unionism . . . and trade-unionism means the ideological enslavement of the workers by the bourgeoisie. Hence, our task, the task of Social-Democracy, is to combat spontaneity, to divert the working-class movement from this spontaneous, trade-unionist striving to come under the wing of the bourgeoisie, and to bring it under the wing of revolutionary Social-Democracy.

It is here that the balance between class and party can be seen to shift decisively away from the class and towards the party. Kautsky's unproblematical formulation of the class – party relationship (whatever may be thought of its merits and demerits) had been converted into a position that might look similar but which was now highly problematical. It was no longer a matter of socialism and the working-class struggle arising 'side by side' and requiring the bridge provided by the party and its theorists. In Lenin's formulation, the proletariat left to itself would not merely fail to develop socialist consciousness but would develop bourgeois consciousness. In other words, this was the *natural* line of development of the proletariat, acting as its 'spontaneous' self, and there were no middle courses available. Thus the task of the party was not to service the class in its necessary development of socialist consciousness but to 'divert' the class from its natural line of development towards bourgeois consciousness. It was the case not merely that (contrary to the views of the 'economists') the economic class struggle was not paramount and would not produce a revolutionary proletariat, but that such economism would issue in a trade-union consciousness that represented the incorporation of the proletariat into existing society and not its revolutionary transcendence. This was the inevitable fate of a class untutored by correct revolutionary theory and deprived of correct revolutionary leadership.

The source of such theory and leadership was the party. It was the party that was now to determine the fate of the class. In the sense that the party still looked to the class as the socialist actor it would be inaccurate to describe this Leninist position in the language of substitutism. However, the terms of the class–party relationship had been altered decisively. The party was now to be seen as the real motor of socialist revolution, the motor that was needed to transport a class that showed every sign (if left to its own devices) of moving in the wrong direction. This had implications for the status and organization of the party. Its status derived from its theoretical credentials in interpreting and applying scientific socialism. As the carrier of correct revolutionary theory the party was the 'real' representative of the proletariat, for it was the party that knew what the proletariat essentially *was* and what was needed for it to 'become what it was'. This required a particular *kind* of party, organized in such a way that the correct theoretical perspective could be translated into effective political leadership. Such a party would not be open and pluralistic, but (especially in Russian conditions) narrow, centralized, and disciplined. Thus the Leninist vanguard party of 'professional revolutionaries' was an authentic expression of a revised view of the kind of intervention that was required if the proletariat was to perform the historical role that Marx had assigned to it. It was also, of course, an indication (and an anticipation) of the authority that could be claimed by a Marxist party on the basis of its superior theoretical knowledge of the real interests of the working class (or 'toiling masses' in later versions). A glance at the experience of the party-states of the twentieth century should be sufficient to dispel any notion that such modes of thinking have been of no more than antiquarian interest.

Not surprisingly, Lenin's version of the class–party relationship has been challenged by other Marxists, both at the time and subsequently. The major contemporary challenge came from Rosa Luxemburg, whose charge against the leadership of the Social Democratic parties and also against Leninism turned on their alleged attempt to replace the spontaneous revolutionary initiative of the class with the organized political leadership of the party. The Leninist party model was to be seen as 'no more or less than a mechanical transference of the Blanquist principles of the organization of conspiratorial groups to the social democratic movement of the working masses'. Luxemburg's attachment to 'spontaneity' did not involve a denial of the role of party, leadership, or organization; but it did involve a repudiation of any position which elevated these above the revolutionary self-organization of the class. It was the *terms* of the class–party relationship that were crucial, and it was necessary frankly to admit that 'errors made by a truly revolutionary labour movement are historically infinitely more fruitful and more valuable than the infallibility of the best of all possible "central committees"'.

Unlike Lenin (and Kautsky), Rosa Luxemburg believed that the proletariat, left to itself, was essentially revolutionary. In strikes and uprisings it gave expression to its nature and destiny. The task, therefore, was to sustain and encourage it in such self-expression, not to stifle it by seeking to force it into an organizational mould. If this view might seem to offer a rather precarious basis for a revolutionary organization (and it is possible to interpret the fate of Luxemburg's Spartacus League in this light), it could nevertheless be presented as an authentic restatement of Marx's own position on the matter. This was not merely Luxemburg's claim, but has been the claim of other Marxists who resist Lenin's version of the class–party relationship. Had not Marx always insisted that (in the words of his Preamble to the *Provisional Rules of the First International)* 'the emancipation of the working classes must be conquered by the working classes themselves'? There could be no mistaking the view held by Marx and Engels that socialism was not merely about the emancipation of the proletariat but rather about its *self*-emancipation. There could therefore be no question of confusing Marxism with Blanquism, or with Leninism. Thus a resort to the texts could provide a reassuring reaffirmation of Marxism as class action against Leninism as party action.

NEW ACTORS, NEW PROBLEMS

The only problem with such reassurance was that it returned the argument to Marx's (philosophical) belief in the essentially revolutionary character of the proletariat, instead of confronting the real implications of Leninism. Clearly a central implication was that the working class might not in practice develop a revolutionary consciousness and would require disciplined tutoring if its role as socialist actor was to be performed. In other words, the question was how the revolution was to be made *despite* the non-revolutionary nature of the working-class movement; and, a further question, how was the proletarian revolution to be made in conditions where the proletariat was not the leading element in society and economy. Lenin had confronted such questions and provided his own answers. A proletarian revolution could be engineered by a proletarian movement that was 'proletarian' in the sense that its theoretical grasp enabled it to understand the objective interests and historical role of the proletariat, even though it was not itself composed of proletarians and despite the fact that the proletariat seemed unaware of the role that history required of it and might not even exist as a developed social formation.

Thus, Lenin explained how Marx's socialist actor could in practice perform its role. Moreover, however troubling the explanation might seem to the exponents of classical Marxism, it at least drew upon some relevant (if also troubling) evidence from the real world. This evidence revealed the difficulties in any attempt simply to read off class behaviour from class position, or to believe that the process whereby the latter would issue in a particular expression of the former was either necessary or straightforward. Instead of a progressive development of proletarian homogeneity and consciousness, Lenin identified a process of incorporation of the western working class into bourgeois society and the role in this process of a working-class sectionalism in the form of a labour aristocracy and of a reformist social democratic leadership. Moreover, in identifying the character of socialist revolution in Russian conditions, Lenin not only emphasized the central role of the party as the proxy-proletariat but also identified the important role of other actors, notably the peasants and the nationalities. Furthermore, when the working class of the West failed to respond to the signal from Russia that the imperialist chain was broken (a response that Lenin's theorization of the revolution had insisted would be forthcoming, his own previous account of the degenerative character of the western working-class movement notwithstanding), Lenin extended the cast of socialist actors to include all the oppressed peoples of the world who were the victims of western imperialism: 'We now stand, not only as the representatives of the proletarians of all countries but as representatives of the oppressed peoples as well.'

Here, then, was the decisive moment of extension, and disintegration, of a traditional socialist cast list. The party-as-proletariat would lead the oppressed masses of the world against their imperialist exploiters in the West. Global revolution was still assured, but its agency was no longer to be seen as the working class of western capitalism but the masses of 'the revolutionary and nationalist East'. In a significant sense the working class of developed capitalism was now to be counted on the side of imperialism, requiring a new version of emancipation from without. However, this was ensured (as Lenin explained) by the global balance of forces:

> In the last analysis, the outcome of the struggle will be determined by the fact that Russia, India, China etc., account for the overwhelming majority of the population of the globe. And during the past few years it is the majority that has been drawn into the struggle for emancipation with extraordinary rapidity, so that in this respect there cannot be the slightest doubt what the final outcome of the world struggle will be. In this sense, the complete victory of socialism is fully and absolutely assured.

The denouement remained the same, but the stage was now set for new socialist actors in new roles, and in new theatres of revolution.

Thus the twentieth-century shift in the centre of gravity of socialism, first signalled in 1917 and further evidenced subsequently, carried with it a profound alteration in socialist thought and practice on the matter of agency. The vocabulary of Marxism might remain, but the 'proletariat' became a metaphor in situations where the party substituted for its absence. This was the case in China, where the Communists mobilized the peasants in a mass movement of national populism. There has developed a considerable roll call of 'national communisms', as 'class' has fused with 'people' in assorted anti-imperialist and modernizing doctrines. Some theorists of national communism (like Fanon and Cabral) have not only substituted the poor peasantry for the industrial proletariat as the truly revolutionary class, but have also discarded Marxism in their general rejection of the western cultural tradition. 'We looked for the working class', wrote Cabral, 'and did not find it.' It is hardly surprising that when an exponent of classical Marxism (like George Lichtheim) cast a critical eye over the ideological assortment of Maoism, Castroism, African socialism, and the rest it produced a bout of theoretical despair:

> Nationalism is identified with socialism, the peasantry with the prolet-ariat, anti-imperialism with anti-capitalism, until all the distinctions painfully elaborated in Marxist literature for a century are cast overboard in favour of a simple dichotomy: western imperialism versus the starving masses of the Third World.

When Marx had identified the proletariat as the carrier of socialism, it was also an identification of the kind of socialism that would be created through its agency. It was a socialism that would inherit the cultural and economic capital of the era it transcended. Thus the grounds upon which the theoretical leaders of Second International Marxism indicted the Bolshevik revolution (wrong actor, wrong time, wrong place) were also linked to a grim foreboding about the kind of regime that would result. To the extent that Marxism, in Leninist and subsequent variants, has been deployed as the theoretical (and organizational) basis of assorted popular movements of economic justice, modernization, and independence, the foreboding may be generalized into wider twentieth-century terms. Some-times this is described as the tragedy of Marxism (nice theory, nasty world). Yet this is surely to indict the world of practice for not behaving as the world of theory decreed. Of course, classical Marxism was not distinguished by its theoretical modesty. It had solved the riddle of history, a theoretical accomplishment to be given practical demonstration through the agency of the working class of developed capitalism.

There was no difficulty, therefore, in showing why the peasantry had no role as socialist actors, or why petty nationalisms would be swallowed up by the development of the international economy and its associated class cleavages, or why the western working class was necessarily the revolu-tionary socialist subject. But of course there should have been such difficulties. Something has already been said about the character of Marx's original identification of the proletariat as socialist actor, but this identi-fication was rooted in a view of the wage-labour – capital relationship as the basic determinant of social reality through the class action it generated. However, why should class position generate class action of a particular kind? And why should a general theory about the nature of social determination provide a reliable guide to the actual forms and consequences that such determination might give rise to? More fundamental still, why should the class antagonisms associated with the mode of production be regarded as of singular determining importance compared with the manifest antagonisms generated by racial, ethnic, religious, sexual, and other conflicts?

If such questions could be ignored by nineteenth-century Marxism, they at least have to be confronted by Marxists (along with everybody else) at the end of the twentieth century. For example, in 1848 the founders of Marxism could confidently predict the socialization of the nation; but a century later it already seemed more plausible to record (in E. H. Carr's phrase) the 'nationalisation of socialism'. It might be recalled that Marx announced the resolution of the national question in class terms at the very moment in European history at which nationalism gave notice that it was unlikely to be content with such subordinate and derivative status. At the end of the twentieth century, with communisms recently dead and nationalisms vibrantly alive, the status reversal stands confirmed. The failure of the western working class to behave in the way expected of it has naturally been seen as a major theoretical problem, along with the ability of the party to substitute itself for the (determining) class in the twentieth-century party-states. There arose in response and consequence a new Marxism of the 'superstructure', sometimes (as with Marcuse) with grimly pessimistic conclusions about the prospects for working-class consciousness and action, but in other hands (as with some of Gramsci's recent disciples) with a more optimistic scenario in which, serviced by its 'organic' intellectuals, a project of working-class cultural hegemony becomes possible. In general, though, the problem has still been framed in formal Marxist terms as that of accounting for the disparity between class position and class behaviour. Yet in this form the problem derives from the terms in which it is discussed, and produces the spectacle of so many recent Marxists boxing their way out of corners they need not have been in. It is possible to admire the deft footwork involved while regretting the needless expenditure of so much effort.

In Marxist terms, much of the responsibility for the failure of the working class in the West to 'become what it is' lies with the social democratic parties and their leaderships. The charge against twentieth-century social democracy is that it has betrayed the working class through its parliamentarism and reformism and has therefore to be regarded as 'objectively' on the side of the existing order despite its ideological veneer and notwithstanding its majority support amongst the working class. This charge was first framed by Lenin (who, it might be recalled, also explained how the British Labour Party was not a proletarian party despite its actual working-class composition, whereas the Bolshevik party was a proletarian party despite the absence of the proletariat in its ranks); it became the orthodoxy of the communist parties; and remains basic to much contemporary *marxisant* analysis. While it is clearly the case, to put the matter briefly, that social democracy has often shown itself prone to accept the standing invitation from capitalist democracy to degenerate into mere electoralism and a permanent accommodation with the existing order, it is also the case that (at some times and in some places) it has demonstrated an ability not merely to resist this invitation but to press some of its own definitions on to the wider society. At this point the argument becomes familiar, and always inconclusive. The Marxist charge against social democracy for betraying the working class into bourgeois reformism is met by the social democratic counter-charge that it operates with people as they are in conditions of political democracy. The argument is unlikely to become fruitful while the 'objective' role of social democracy, always and everywhere, is proclaimed as an article of faith by those whose belief in the 'essentially' revolutionary and self-emancipating capacities of the working class remains disconcertingly untroubled by the ease with which those capacities can evidently be thwarted by social democratic politicians (as well as by Leninist parties).

FROM CLASS TO PEOPLE

In important respects, of course, the social democratic tradition (in its generic post-1917 sense, which includes those non-communist and, usually, non-Marxist positions that have preferred to describe themselves as democratic socialist) has wanted to give its own account of socialism's actors. While rooted in the organized working-class movement, it has wanted to match the universality of the socialist idea with a movement that reflected this universality. Thus, even during the Second International period, when Marxist orthodoxy proclaimed the proletariat as the universal class, Jaurès preferred to present the socialist party as 'the geometrical locus of all great causes and all great ideas'. Marxism had conjoined the idea and the interest, the universal and the particular, so that socialism was to be seen *as* the victory of working-class interest. Democratic socialists refused this formulation, in favour of a position that combined working-class interest *with* socialism. The universality of the latter should not be reduced to the particularism of the former. The working class, as the exploited class of capitalism, would be the main beneficiary of socialism and the natural basis of a mass socialist party, but it should not be identified with socialism. Such an identification would be wrong in both principle and practice.

It would be wrong in principle because socialism was at bottom a matter of values and therefore accessible to anyone capable of making a moral choice, and because the Marxist habit of dealing only in class categories left too little 'space' for individual human beings. It would be wrong in practice because of the flawed social analysis that sustained it. A united, revolutionary class of enlightened socialists was an unlikely development of a working class that had been degraded and sectionalized by capitalism. As Bernard Shaw put it, 'such an army of light is no more to be gathered from the human product of nineteenth century civilisation than grapes are to be gathered from thistles'. Moreover, it was an illusion to believe that capitalist crisis served to radicalize the working class; just as it was an illusion to believe that class polarization was underway when all the evidence pointed to increasing class differentiation and the creation of new, intermediate groupings. The conclusion from all this, on grounds of both principle and policy, was that there was a need to construct a socialist movement of persuasion and reform capable of a wide appeal to people in different social classes.

In Britain, the early Fabians directed their appeal to the *nouveau couche sociale* of administrators, professionals, and technicians; while R. H. Tawney, combining Fabian rationalism and socialist moralism, advised the Labour Party of the need to look less like a defender of the sectional interests of the trade unions in order to appeal to all those people 'whose business in life is not snatching at profits, but constructive activity' (though this was 'not a question . . . of giving a second place to the claims of the industrial workers, who are capitalism's chief victims, but of presenting those claims as what in essence they are, a demand for a life that is worthy of human beings, and which no decent man will withhold from his fellows'). In framing the socialist argument in this way, it was possible to tap radical and patriotic traditions and harness them to the socialist cause. Within English socialism, for example, there has been a strong undercurrent of sentiment relating to a 'real' England, a people's England (what Orwell described as 'the England that is only just beneath the surface'), and an attempt to mobilize this England for socialist purposes. Socialism could be identified with social solidarity and so made the basis for a common culture rooted in shared beliefs. This approach came to distinguish Swedish socialism in particular, after its disengagement from Marxism, and was central to the thought of key figures such as Ernst Wigforss and Per Albin Hansson, the latter coining the metaphor of the 'people's home' to describe the socialist vision of a good society. In general, then, while the communist parties traditionally operated within a class perspective that issued in a stance of workerism, the social democratic parties have sought to combine a base in the organized labour movement with a more generalized appeal. In its 1959 Bad Godesberg programme, the German SPD formalized what this involved: 'From the party of the working class the Social Democratic Party has become a party of the people.'

However, in this particular version of social democratic substitutism, of 'people' for 'class', the casualty seemed to some to be not merely one kind of socialism but *any* kind of serious socialism. It was perhaps not just a case of new actors, but of a different play. This could be presented as an authentic response to the deradicalization of an embourgeoisified working class and the increasing significance of new social groups. This points attention to the importance attached to the changing class structure of Western Europe in contemporary socialist positions on the matter of agency. Some socialists identified a 'new' working class attached to consumer capitalism and drew conservative conclusions; while other socialists found a 'new' class of technical workers raising issues of power and control and came up with a radical scenario. There have also been assorted attempts to find surrogates for the traditional proletariat on the Left, though often (most conspicuously with the student 'revolution' of the 1960s) still reflecting a belief in the need to attach themselves at some point to socialism's historical actor and sleeping giant. While some socialists have sought to assemble a rainbow coalition of the differently dispossessed, others have emphasized the task of winning support among the newly possessed.

All this may be taken as evidence of the contemporary crisis of agency within socialism. Attempts to retain the 'working class' as socialist actor, in the face of this crisis produced by its failure to act in the way expected of it, are reflected in the attention given to what Poulantzas has called the 'boundary problem' in socialist class analysis. On the one hand, the boundary of the modern working class is drawn so expansively that socialism no longer has to rely upon the agency of the traditional proletariat. On the other hand, the boundary is drawn so narrowly (as it is by Poulantzas himself) that the working class shrinks to such diminutive proportions that any socialist strategy must clearly involve alliances with other social groups. In this way class analysis carries with it direct strategic implications for socialism. Indeed, it is *intended* to, as is evident from the kind of class analysis that was developed by the Eurocommunists to sustain their position of a 'popular alliance' between the working class and other social forces. An echo of this position, based upon a similar analysis of changing class patterns, was heard in Britain through the agency of Eric Hobsbawm, whose *The Forward March of Labour Halted?* (1981) provided a major focus for strategic debate on the Left. It is scarcely surprising that, from within the Marxist tradition itself as well as from outside it, the question was asked whether the Eurocommunist position did not really mark the abandonment of socialism's self-emancipating actor rather than its retention and redefinition. Moreover, if it did mean this, did it not also mark the replacement of 'class' by 'people' and, thereby, the abandonment of the basic Marxist position concerning the centrality of the class struggle between capital and labour as the fundamental antagonism within society?

This raised problems for the orthodox Marxists, but it need not raise problems for other socialists. Unless socialism is defined in terms of the victory of a class, itself defined in terms of the relationship between wage labour and capital, the failure of that class to perform its necessary revolutionary or historic role does not do fatal damage to the socialist project. What would do fatal damage would be the inability of socialist parties to assemble new constituencies of support in the 'new times' associated with the fracturing of old class lines, which is why the issue of agency lies at the centre of contemporary socialist politics. There is no reason to expect the traditional working class to be the single carrier of socialism. Indeed, there is some reason to expect that the old working class (for example, in its attachment to such shibboleths as 'free collective bargaining') will reflect and reproduce the rationality of capitalism rather than challenge it fundamentally. It is a major achievement of feminism not merely to have identified the limited stereotype of socialism's traditional actor (male, manual, muscular) but to have identified the limited character of the wage labour-capital relationship that underpinned it. Feminism has extended and enriched the definition of the socialist project, from 'work' to 'life', and has extended the range of possible socialist actors in the process.

'One can say', writes Bauman, 'that the history of socialism has come full circle. It started . . . as an idea in search of a constituency; it has become recently a constituency in search of an idea.' The constituency consists of all those people in search of a more rational, secure, and human way of ordering society (which includes, of course, their own lives and communities) than that offered by late-twentieth-century global capitalism. If this constituency has had difficulty in making connections with socialism, it might be argued (and is here) that this is related to the kinds of socialism that have been on offer and to the traditionally limited definition of socialism's agents. When André Gorz identifies a 'non-class of non-producers' as the leading actors of a post-industrial socialism this might seem to represent the final dissolution of any coherent socialist strategy; or it might be taken to indicate the radical implications of recasting the socialist project in such a way that a general project requires a general subject. Marx framed the socialist project in terms of a universal humanism but tied it to a single class, fighting on a single front. The crisis occasioned by the failure of this actor to perform as expected might yet enable socialism to find a base as broad as its prospectus. Moreover, as Bahro has said, 'the way leading out of the present situation need not be conceived as "socialism" by all who want to tread it.'

7 Futures

Socialism is dead.

(Alain Touraine)

Socialism is only a possible future.

(Tom Bottomore)

The problem with being a socialist at the end of the twentieth century is that the rest of the century has already happened. If the nineteenth century taught some powerful lessons about the nature of capitalism to set against its own self-image, the twentieth century has performed a similar service in relation to socialism. In many respects it has been socialism's century. On one view, this became a story of victory and vindication. On another view, however, it was a journey into dismay and disintegration. As Bauman describes it, in *Socialism: The Active Utopia*, 'the two centuries of modern socialism's history extend from its majestic advent in the attire of utopia to the incapacitation arising from its alleged realisation.'

THEN AND NOW

Consider the contrast between the socialist world of 1900 and that of today. In 1900 there were no socialist countries, but a confident expectation that there soon would be. Both Marxists and Fabians conscripted history to their side, and presented socialism as the necessary outcome of a process of economic development. The Marxists had a comprehensive science of society which explained why capitalism was destined to collapse under the weight of its own economic contradictions and why a revolutionary proletariat would conquer power and establish a classless society. The Fabians had a historical science which revealed the drive towards collectivism that could be harnessed by reform and reformers to establish a socialist organization of production and distribution. Both Marxists and Fabians, it should be added, assumed that socialism would be constructed upon the economic, political, and cultural foundations of a mature capitalism.

Now, a century on, things look very different. Hundreds of millions of people have lived under socialist regimes around the world, but not one of these regimes even approximated the description of socialism offered at the turn of the century by either revolutionaries or reformers. The reformist perspective, of the western working class voting its way to socialism, seems to have ground to a halt in the shifting sands of a social democracy that has found it increasingly difficult to deliver even on the limited goal of welfare capitalism. The revolutionary perspective has of course fared even less well in the West, owing to the persistent refusal of its chosen actors to perform their historical role. The success of socialist revolution elsewhere, from 1917 onwards, created the authoritarian party-state as the twentieth-century representative of 'actually existing socialism', until its seismic disintegration in 1989. At the beginning of the twentieth century Marxism could present itself in terms of a universal humanism; at the end of the twentieth century it had to confront the fact that every Marxist state had been a dictatorship. This may be a necessary fact (as its critics argue) or a contingent fact (as its friends suggest), but it is a decisive fact in explaining the salience that 'socialism' had come to have for the populations of western capitalism.

At this point it would seem plausible to settle into a conclusion of the following kind. A reformist socialism had established itself as the appropriate form of socialism in the countries of capitalist democracy, but had become less able to deliver social democracy. A revolutionary socialism had shown itself to be appropriate to other societies, but only in an authoritarian form. In this sense, early-century socialists in Western Europe were correct in tying their version of socialism to general economic and social development. However, they were wrong in believing that such development would necessarily issue in socialism, whether through revolution or reform, and in disbelieving that other versions of socialism were available where their preconditions were absent. They were prisoners of their own theory, especially when they dressed it up as science, which is why the recalcitrant world of practice was always capable of taking them so much by surprise.

The conclusion just stated is not merely plausible in terms of the evident connection between kinds of socialisms and kinds of societies, but also corresponds to the twentieth-century organization of rival socialist camps. An authoritarian communism (East) confronted a reformist social democracy (West). In the socialist world cup, the match between the Soviet Union and Sweden was played out for much of this century, and looked likely to continue into the next century until the dramatic Soviet collapse towards the end of the second half (when Sweden's long embrace of social democracy also ruptured). Here, then, is an important part of the twentieth-century dilemma of western socialism. The century's first lesson seemed to be that there were only two choices on the Left, between an undemocratic communism and an unsocialist social democracy. If this was indeed the choice, then it was hardly surprising that western workers (and many socialists) should settle for social democracy and decline invitations to embark on a more perilous course. They had more to lose than their chains, and this 'more' included the political freedoms and democratic rights that they had struggled so long and hard to achieve. As Lichtheim puts it: 'social democracy might be boring, but at least it was familiar and held no menace to freedom and decency.'

The socialist credentials of the social democrats might be disputed, and the degenerative tendencies of social democratic parties in office might be acknowledged, but their democratic credentials were sound. They could therefore brush aside the guilt-by-association smears from the Right on this score, while the charge of 'electoralism' levelled against them from the Left could be taken as confirmation of their democratic sensibilities. Their commitment to socialism might be uncertain, or postponed to an indefinite future, but not so their commitment to democracy. In so far as the twentieth century had suggested at least the possibility that there might be a trade-off between socialism and political freedom (and certainly that, contrary to an earlier prospectus, there was no necessary connection between socialism and political freedom), the working class of the West sensibly preferred to err on the side of political freedom. This option was, of course, made more attractive by the ability of social democracy to combine democracy with welfare, by extracting reforms and improvements from capitalism on a continuing basis. Such reformism was already the practical policy of pre-1914 social democracy, despite its Marxist camouflage, and became the explicit basis of later social democratic politics. Its golden age, confused at the time with eternity, was the quarter century of the postwar 'settlement' after 1945 when capitalism boomed and social democracy prospered.

It was the need to make an accommodation with the political facts of life in Western Europe that also moved the communist parties in a 'Euro-communist' direction. This direction was unmistakably towards social democracy, and involved a repudiation of an earlier Leninism with its dismissal of 'bourgeois' democracy. It is true that Eurocommunist protestations of faith in the institutions of parliamentary democracy and repudiation of the revolutionary road were matched with equally loud protestations that there was no ideological dilution of a social democratic kind involved in this process; but the *direction* of change was clear enough. If Carrillo, one of the architects of Eurocommunism, insisted that 'there cannot be any confusion between "Eurocommunism" and social democracy in the ideological sphere' because the former 'proposes to *transform* capitalist society not to *administer* it', this could not conceal the adoption of a position which at the beginning of the century would have been regarded as a clear endorsement of 'revisionism'. The subsequent history of the western communist parties merely confirmed this, sometimes (as in Italy) marking their terminal decline with a final and formal social democratic embrace.

However, if Eurocommunism had endeavoured to shed some of its political problems by moving in a social democratic direction, it had thereby also acquired the contemporary problems of social democracy itself. The Eurocommunists might claim that they really *meant* it when they said they were in the business of reforming their way to socialism (unlike the social democrats, who merely said it), but this by itself was scarcely enough to sustain an effective socialist reformism. If Eurocommunism was a reflection of the historic problems of the communist tradition in the West, the social democratic tradition confronted major difficulties of its own. This is why the earlier comfortable conclusion about a social democratic reformism having established itself as the appropriate form of socialism in the West turns out to be rather too comfortable. If a first lesson of the century seemed to be that the only choice on the left was between an undemocratic communism and an unsocialist social democracy, the second and more alarming lesson seemed to be that even the social democratic option was becoming less available.

DILEMMAS OF SOCIAL DEMOCRATS

The strategy of social democracy has been to milk the capitalist cow, an activity that has continued steadily if erratically through the twentieth century. Its fruits are to be seen in the growth of protective legislation and welfare provision that constitutes the history of social policy in this period (and which, in historical terms, represents a major advance in the security of working-class life). In the mid-century heyday of social democracy it was possible to believe that this process would continue in uninterrupted fashion. The socialist milk would continue to flow in abundance from the capitalist cow. Indeed, upon the basis of this belief it seemed plausible to claim that traditional socialist objectives (defined in terms of welfare and social equality) could be achieved without the traditional socialist means (social ownership of the means of production). Welfare capitalism could be made to deliver the social goods that 'socialism' had traditionally stood for and which 'socialists' had formerly believed could be achieved only through the abolition of private ownership of the means of production. The *locus classicus* of this confident social democratic revisionism is Crosland's *The Future of Socialism*, written in the mid-1950s, with its admiring glances towards the social democratic parties in Germany and Sweden, where old ideological baggage was being tossed overboard (to beneficial electoral effect).

It is clear now that this position rested upon a view of modern capitalism that was too benign and domesticated. It did not take account of the dynamic of inequality within capitalism that was serving to increase inequality rather than to diminish it, even (as Titmuss showed at the time, and as has been amply confirmed since) through the organization of welfare itself. In other words, traditional socialist objectives were *not* being achieved, even though there was a general increase in social welfare and living standards. Thus it was a matter not merely of revising socialist *means*, but of redefining socialist *ends* as well. This was the option taken by some social democrats, involving a historic adjustment of ambitions in the direction of what capitalism could actually deliver and the renunciation of larger purposes. The formation of the Social Democratic Party in Britain in the 1980s might, perhaps, be taken as a formal declaration of this kind. If capitalism could not deliver equality, then the social democrats would settle for what it could deliver and carry on milking as best they could.

This points to a fundamental characteristic, and difficulty, of the social democratic tradition in general. Much of its efforts have been concerned with making alterations to the pattern of distribution under capitalism, through an extractive politics of reform and concession. However, this kind of distributional politics has been most successful during periods of capitalist buoyancy and growth, and least successful during periods of capitalist crisis and contraction. In other words, it represents a politics of *dependency* rather than of change and transformation. The long postwar capitalist boom was therefore also the period when social democracy was most confident and successful, while the collapse of this period of expansion has brought with it a crisis for social democracy. Indeed, at such times the achievements of social democracy in terms of welfare provisions and protections against unrestrained market capitalism can be presented by capitalist 'common sense' as an incubus that is preventing the economic system from performing effectively according to its own internal dynamics. The logic of this argument has been deployed to good effect by the contemporary New Right in the context of economic recession and global competition, while the social democratic Left has found it difficult to mount a credible resistance or alternative when what was needed was not a dependent strategy of distribution but a convincing strategy of production.

This suggests a more general organizational and theoretical vulnerability on the part of social democracy. Its method was reform and its instrument was the state. The effect was that it piled ever more powers and responsibilities upon the state but without giving much serious thought to the organizational problems of social democracy in terms of control, autonomy, and accountability. The vision of the welfare society thus turned into the bureaucratic apparatus of the welfare state. Centralism and uniformity triumphed over decentralism and diversity. A socialism of self-government was lost in an administrative collectivism. Social ownership turned into state ownership. This is put too baldly and without the necessary qualifications, but it forms part of the recent crisis of social democracy. Not merely has the extractive, distributional strategy of social democracy been disabled by the harsher economic climate that followed the end of the long postwar boom, but its attachment to the state (in circumstances where people do not experience the state as 'their' state) has made it vulnerable to libertarian arguments about freedom, choice, and autonomy. Thus, in both East and West, twentieth-century socialism has come to be associated with statism and bureaucracy rather than with democratic self-government, and this has produced a marked disinclination on the part of western electorates to believe that it is desirable to extend a socialism of distribution into a socialism of production. As these electorates have also become more variegated, with a declining inclination to pay the taxes necessary to fund the social democratic state, it is not that the extension of social democratic ambitions has proved more intractable but that extension has been replaced by contraction.

If all this reflects the contemporary difficulties of social democracy, it also reflects the reason why this tradition cannot stand still. If one option is to throw the towel in and make a final accommodation with market liberalism, another option is to attempt a redefinition of theory and strategy. This was evident in the radicalization of social democratic parties in Europe that took place in the 1970s and early 1980s, equivalent to the deradical- ization that occurred a generation earlier, just as it is evident in the new revisionism that has followed in its wake. This is also why the character- ization of the 'objective' nature of social democracy traditionally offered by the Marxist tradition is scarcely adequate. Indeed, Marxism's own difficulties in recent years are apparent enough. At the beginning of this century there was a comprehensive, scientific Marxism; towards the end of the century there developed a whole range of Marxisms. There has been both a 'revival' of Marxism and a 'crisis' of Marxism. At the beginning of the century the intellectual leaders of European Marxism were also the leaders of the Second International parties and of an advancing political practice; at the end of the century they are, at best, the practitioners of a 'Professorial Marxism' (Parkin's phrase) of the closet and the learned journal, and of a receding political practice. Moreover, the focus of much recent Marxism has shifted significantly. As McLellan points out, 'whereas Marx started with philosophy and moved to economics, the typical thinkers of Western Marxism have moved in the opposite direction'.

THE MIRAGE OF MARXISM

In significant respects this century has seen the collapse of the whole pack of cards that constituted classical Second International Marxism. This doctrinal collapse long predated the collapse in 1989 of those regimes constructed upon its orthodoxies. The failure of proletarian internationalism in 1914, followed by the triumph of Bolshevism in 1917, gave early indication that events would not bow to the requirements of Marxist science. The implications of this for Marxist theory remained for a long time unexplored as Marxism itself was appropriated by the communists and served up in an authorized version. The renewed vitality of Marxism in the West from the 1960s to the 1980s derived from its escape from the clutches of communist orthodoxy, and the infusion of elements from Marx's work that were unrecognized before 1917 (when 'Marxism' consisted essentially of *Capital* plus Engels) and suppressed after 1917. However, much of this intellectual vitality was directed towards problems of Marxism's own making. Capitalism had not collapsed, class polarization had not intensified, a revolutionary proletariat had not emerged. How was this to be explained? Further, there was the problem of the socialist party-states of Eastern Europe, where the abolition of private ownership of the means of production had conspicuously not delivered an end to political and economic inequality and oppression. Thus, this new Marxism was to be found wrestling with ever-increasing opaqueness with a formulation of 'base' and 'superstructure' that retained some significant meaning to the determining character of the mode of production, while emphasizing the role of the ideological sphere in explaining the ability of capitalism to maintain itself without coercion in conditions of political democracy.

Indeed, modern Marxism might be seen as offering its own gloomy commentary on the prospects for socialism in the West. Once it is acknowledged that Marx presented the most penetrating theorization of the workings of capitalism that socialism has produced but in the absence of a serious political theory went on to draw wholly unwarranted conclusions from it regarding the future of socialism (conclusions upon which later Marxists were to bestow scientific status), it is not surprising that so much of recent Marxism has been preoccupied with the failure of history to deliver the goods.

Following Lenin, social democracy has been identified by the Marxists and *marxisants* as playing a key role in this process, which seems (to put it moderately) to rest upon a somewhat exaggerated view of the ability of social democratic politicians to mislead a class so completely about the nature of its own real interests. More generally, the 'problem' of the durability of capitalist democracy increasingly came to be treated in terms of the ideological hegemony of capitalism. Much juggling with ideological state apparatuses and the like has been engaged in to conceptualize the process whereby this hegemony is sustained. In some versions it becomes difficult to see how such an ideological stranglehold could ever be broken (and, indeed, some twentieth-century Marxists have delivered this final, morbid verdict on the prospects for socialism).

As ever, then, Marxists continue to be able to *explain* what is going on: for example, why capitalism is doomed, and why it is not; why the working class is revolutionary, and why it is not; and so on. This claim to superior knowledge continues to distinguish 'Marxists' from other kinds of social-ists, who cannot, it seems, see beyond their moralistic and reformist noses. Vulgar Marxists know that the class struggle is alive and well and the socialist revolution is just around the next capitalist corner, if only the social democrats who are blocking the path can be pushed out of the way. Professorial Marxism can explain why this is not, exactly, the case. Either way, contemporary Marxism in the West, if this term does not suggest an entity too coherent and alive, seems vastly better at explaining the world than at changing it (which, as Marx once pointed out, is really the point).

In the face of this daunting ideological superstructure, perhaps a small dose of simple-mindedness is in order. It may not, after all, really be so surprising that the electorates of the West have demonstrated an attachment to capitalist democracy and a reluctance to embrace a socialist (as opposed to a social democratic) alternative. Further, it may be that this has rather less to do with the ideological properties of capitalism than with the revealed properties of socialism. After all, it has been possible during the twentieth century to learn something about the character of the available alternatives to capitalist democracy. The electorates of Western Europe have been able to observe societies where private ownership of the means of production has been eliminated and to compare such societies with their own. They have learnt, contrary to the assurances of early-century socialists, that it is quite possible to combine socialism with political despotism. They know that communist parties that proclaim their faith in liberal democracy have also been apologists for Stalinism. The simple-minded point is that the future of socialism clearly depends upon the ability of socialists to *persuade* the majority of citizens in the capitalist democracies that they are genuinely offering more, not less, better, not worse, and that they evidence some plausible grounds for believing that they could actually deliver on their offer.

This suggests the need for socialists to devote at least as much time and energy to the task of constructing a convincing account of socialism as to the more familiar task of denouncing, analysing, and exposing capitalism. It is, after all, the nature of the *alternative* to capitalist democracy that is at issue, since there are demonstrably worse alternatives. Indeed, it is the nature of the alternative to one *form* of capitalist democracy (the deregulated and divisive neo-liberal form) that is the contemporary challenge. Marx, it will be recalled, brushed aside all such preoccupations as recipe-writing for the cookshops of the future, a pointless exercise that should be left in the capable historical hands of future socialist cooks. In general, socialists have been more than ready to take their lead from Marx in this matter. This is no longer a tenable position, if ever it was. There is more that needs to be said about socialism than that it is non-capitalism. Even if some of the recipes have to be taken on trust, people rightly want to know something about the organization of the socialist kitchen and, where possible, to test the heat.

Socialism's failure in this respect has not, of course, been simply an oversight or omission. That would be serious enough, but it is made more serious because it has derived from a particular kind of analysis (again exemplified by Marxism). An argument that says that capitalism is the source of every social problem (even, in some versions, of every *personal* problem) extends naturally into an assumption that such problems will not, by definition, exist under socialism, or even that *no* significant problems will exist under socialism. Thus it can be claimed that the end of capitalism will also mean the abolition of the state, power, and politics ('properly so-called'), a claim that is definitionally true in the context of the theory from which it derived, has been taken literally by its adherents (most vividly by Lenin), and is simply incredible. It is a matter of some significance that socialism's dominant theoretical tradition (i.e. Marxism) has traditionally lacked any serious political theory, since politics is to be regarded as ('essentially') a matter of something else. More recent Marxist wriggling with the 'relative autonomy' of the state may be seen as an attempt to get off that particular hook.

Against this sort of background, then, it is not surprising if late-twentieth-century socialism has acquired a somewhat serious credibility problem. This may also explain why so much socialist argument in the recent past has seemed to consist of socialists talking to, and writing for, each other in a private language, and so little of it to be an exercise in public persuasion. If there was ever a time when socialism as theory could remain unsullied and untouched by events, that time has long since passed (or should have done). There remain, of course, those socialists for whom 'socialism' stands as the unexplored and unexplorable answer to things as they are. The word is still sometimes used as if it possessed magical properties capable of dissolving every problem to which it is applied. The story is told of the advice tendered by the old hand to the aspiring Labour politician facing his first selection meeting. When asked what sort of housing policy he was in favour of, he should reply that he was in favour of a 'socialist' housing policy. Ditto for education, health, the economy – and so on.

A socialism of this kind is simply incapable of learning from experience. It will go to its grave muttering its reassuring incantations ('production for use not for profit' etc.) and wondering why nobody seems to be listening very much any more. Its conception of socialism will remain uncontaminated by the experience of actual socialist states, an experience that is judged not to be 'relevant' to its own quintessential socialism or not 'really' to be socialism at all. The fact that there is not a single existing society where 'socialism' is to be found is not thought to raise any problems concerning its own pristine model. It is enough, it seems, to be a resolute anti-capitalist, whether this resolution is displayed in the form of theoretical critique or defensive struggle of a rather more practical kind. Indeed, many socialists are clearly much more comfortable in a role that is essentially negative, oppositional, and defensive. They produce volumes on the nature of capitalist democracy, but little on the character of socialist democracy. They attach themselves to protective struggles of resistance against the economic rationality of capitalism, but in the absence of a developed account of the economics of socialism this often looks more like a defence of the past against the future.

A CREDIBLE SOCIALISM

At the turn of the century, Bernard Shaw described how the conception of socialism held by many contemporary enthusiasts for socialism was really an illusion:

> If the Socialist future were presented in its reality to those who are devoting all the energy they have to spare after their day's work, and all the enthusiasm of which they are capable, to 'the Cause', many of them would not lift a finger for it, and would even disparage and loathe it as a miserably prosaic 'bourgeois' development and extension of the middle class respectability of today. When any part of Socialism presents itself in the raw reality of a concrete proposal, capable of being adopted by a real Government, and carried out by a real Executive, the professed Socialists are the last people in the country who can be depended on to support it.

There is, perhaps, no need for socialism to be *quite* as prosaic and respectable as Shaw's impish Fabianism might suggest. It may not really be necessary to choose to swim with Shaw or drown with William Morris. However, Shaw's point is a real one, and has at least as much force as a commentary on the condition of socialism at the end of the century as at the beginning. Indeed, it finds a direct echo in the interesting discussion of *The*

Politics of Socialism by the political theorist John Dunn, with its central theme of the need for socialists to recognize that 'the best of socialist governments is, in the end, only a government'.

Yet the fact is that many socialists, and kinds of socialism, have managed over the years to avoid the need for this sort of recognition. Socialism becomes synonymous with social harmony. Socialization of the means of production is identified with the abolition of the state and the elimination of all forms of inequality and oppression. A socialism of economic abundance means an end to the politics and economics of scarcity. The rationality of socialist planning replaces the irrationalities of the market. Collective planning coexists with producer self-management. Even human nature itself is transformed, as the new socialist (wo)man steps into the shoes vacated by the old capitalist individualism. Now the point is not so much that socialists should not believe some of these things, but that their socialism should not *depend* upon such beliefs. For example, the new socialist man is regularly discovered at moments of great revolutionary drama. Orwell discovered him (dressed in anarchist clothes) in revolutionary Spain:

> The revolutionary atmosphere remained as I had first known it. General and private, peasant and militia-man, still met as equals; everyone drew the same pay, wore the same clothes, ate the same food, and called everyone else 'thou' and 'comrade'; there was no boss-class, no menial class, no beggars, no prostitutes, no lawyers, no priests, no boot-licking, no cap-touching. I was breathing the air of equality.

It will also be recalled, however, that the main lesson that Orwell brought back from Spain was not that this was the socialist future but that it was a fleeting condition that could be so quickly and mercilessly crushed by a socialism of another, more 'realistic' kind.

The point, then, is that socialists need to look as though they know their way around the world, instead of looking as if they inhabit a world entirely of their own construction. The straitened circumstances in which socialists have found themselves in the closing decades of the twentieth century have certainly been a painful education in this respect; but this learning process still has to wrestle against the inherited mental apparatus of socialism's previous history. A credible socialism would take people as they (more or less) recognizably are, even while hoping for some growth in their social feelings. It would recognize that political life presents permanent problems of theory and organization, and that such problems are not simply the problems of capitalism. This would carry with it a recognition of the need for a state as the arena of collective allocation decisions, and for machinery and procedures whereby such decisions are made. It would acknowledge scarcity as the normal and continuing feature of economic life, requiring decisions and priorities in relation to competing claims on finite resources. It would not exaggerate the superior rationality of comprehensive economic planning and would accept that such planning is neither technically possible nor actually desirable. In this respect, as in others, it would demonstrate a capacity to learn from political and economic experience, not least from the actual experience of twentieth-century socialisms. It would not, of course, pretend that it was a science, or that it could predict the future, or that its coming was inevitable, or that it had solved the riddle of history.

In fact, it might be said that socialists need to know (and to be seen to know) both more and less. They need, in the West at least, to show not only that they understand the matters just mentioned, but that they know how to construct a socialist strategy and programme that looks plausible in terms of the political and economic situation of these societies. This is more difficult than it sounds, and only some socialist rhetoric makes it sound easy. Again, Dunn makes this point well:

> The most serious political doubt about socialist policies in advanced capitalist societies, a doubt now massively grounded in the experience of the populations of these societies wherever socialist politics has had any real success, is whether socialist governments do or can know what they are doing.

Yet they clearly do need to know what they are doing if they are to convince people on a durable basis that they can offer practical solutions to the problems of these societies. Moreover, the setting in which they have to operate is one where capitalism will not be replaced by 'socialism' in an afternoon or a week but where, even if it is replaced at all, it is likely to involve a political process that occupies a span of historical time at least equivalent to the rise of capitalism itself; and in which, certainly when a critical point is reached, there is likely to be resistance of a most determined kind from the capitalist *ancien régime* faced with the loss of its position and privileges. More immediately, the setting is one in which the real choice and struggle are between different kinds of market system and different forms of capitalist democracy.

In this crucial and difficult sense, then, socialists need to know more if socialism is to have a future. In another sense, though, the credibility of socialism depends upon socialists knowing rather less than they have in the past. In part, this involves knowing less about what other people really want or need, less knowledge about their 'real' interest and more 'real' knowledge about their expressed interests. More generally, it involves an infusion of theoretical and historical modesty. At one time it might have been plausible for socialists to claim that they understood everything and could explain everything, a claim founded upon the unique distinction of having cracked the historical code. In particular, this has been the customary claim of the Marxist tradition, and certainly helps to account for its appeal during periods when historical certainty has been in short supply. In the 1930s, for example, it was widely asserted that only Marxism could explain what was going on (a bizarre claim in retrospect, given the damage that fascism and Stalinism were doing to classical Marxist assumptions), and that to be a communist was therefore to be on the side of history and progress. 'I am a communist', declared Stephen Spender, 'because I am a liberal.' That particular god has failed, of course, but the habit of thought behind it is still hard for some socialists to break. They still give the impression of knowing (or thinking they know) more about the historical process than anybody else, which enables them to explain exactly what particular phenomena (like Thatcherism) really 'mean' and 'represent', even if outward appearances suggest otherwise. This frequently enables them to arrive at comforting conclusions (based upon their special ability to detect immanent social trends) to the effect that history is still on course even though this may not be immediately apparent to the untutored eye.

In the past, this claim to superior knowledge has seemed a source of strength for socialism. It is now disabling, both because it is no longer believed and because the twentieth century has taught some sharp lessons about those who ground their claim to political power in the claimed possession of special theoretical and historical knowledge. This does not mean, of course, that socialism has not advanced our understanding of long-term social causation through its analysis of the mode of production, but it does mean that it has extended its legitimate claim to this kind of knowledge into illegitimate claims to other kinds of knowledge (about *how* shaping trends will be mediated in practice and action). Thus, there were good analytical grounds for believing that the collapse of the long postwar economic boom and the associated collapse of working-class expectations would provide an important opening to the Left. So neo-Marxists confidently constructed a scenario in which capitalism was on course for a major 'legitimation crisis'. What the analysis had more difficulty in anticipating was the New Right's skilful political revival of economic liberalism and the fact that in Britain the Labour Party should decide that this was the appropriate time to attempt political suicide. Socialists need, therefore, to evidence somewhat more understanding of such matters as historical contingency, luck, unintended consequences, and political skill than they have evidenced in the past. This requires a certain modesty; but they do, after all, have rather a lot to be modest about.

BETWEEN PAST AND FUTURE

At the end of the twentieth century, then, socialism is not to be regarded as inevitable, omniscient, or uniform; but is it to be regarded as dead? Does it belong to yesterday rather than to tomorrow? To the old millenium but not to the new? In some respects it clearly does carry the marks of its nineteenth-century origins, as in its putative historical codebreaking, its confident progressivism in relation to social change, its pseudo-scientism, and its identification of a class formed in the heyday of industrial capitalism as the agency of change. It is not surprising that there has been some twentieth-century reckoning with elements of this nineteenth-century intellectual kitbag. On one view, this reckoning has produced fatal consequences for the whole socialist project, leaving it stranded between a recently deceased authoritarian statism as the twentieth-century form of actually existing socialism and a western labour movement distinguished by a negative 'labourism' organized around the defence of sectional interests at a time when post-industrial capitalism is anyway kicking away the supports of a traditional class structure. Tom Bottomore wrote,

> It may be that the word 'socialism' has become so corrupted by its association with authoritarian regimes, with centralised planning, with the obsessive pursuit of technological innovation and economic growth, as to be unsuitable any longer to describe the objectives of movements of liberation in the late twentieth century.

However, there remain reasons for believing that the obituary notices for socialism in the West may at least be premature. In so far as socialism began life, and found its common thread, in a critique of an unregulated and socially irresponsible capitalism, there is a real sense in which socialism is still at the point at which it came in (except that the critique of this kind of capitalism has now to be coupled with a critique of certain kinds of 'socialism'). Unless it is believed that capitalism has ceased to be vulnerable to the arguments traditionally levelled against it, there is no reason to think that the socialist project is exhausted. At the end of the twentieth century, no less than at the beginning of the nineteenth century, a system of private ownership of the means of economic production and market exchange that refuses to accept wider social obligations continues to lack a justificatory moral principle, and its operation continues to produce economic conditions and distributional consequences that are damaging and unequal. It continues, therefore, to be vulnerable to socialist values and to socialist analysis, and socialism remains as the pole around which an alternative system of social and economic organization can be framed. The poor remain poor and the unequal remain unequal *because* of actions taken by the rich to maintain their position. Opportunities for the many are restricted *because* they are appropriated by the few. Economic failure and social dislocation arise *because* social justice and solidarity are neglected. In global terms, the South stays poor *because* the North uses its power to stay rich. Both domestically and internationally, capitalism continues to solve its problems by inflicting its 'externalities' upon other people, and as an economic system it remains anarchic and unplanned. Socialism has represented the historical attempt to harness economic life to the test of social values and social reason, and there seems every reason to think that it will continue in this role for as long as people go on wanting to put their societies into a more morally satisfactory and rational shape.

Indeed, it could scarcely be argued that there is less *need* for socialism in the condition of the world at the end of the twentieth century. Technological change threatens to deliver economic and social consequences which, if left to the private determination of the market, seem set to produce casualties of an intolerable and almost unimaginable kind. The attempt to manage economic and social change on this scale, involving radical redefinitions of work and non-work and their distributional implications, is both daunting and pressing. The suggestion that it can safely be left 'to the market' is genuinely frightening. The social disintegration and *malaise* of western societies is already sufficiently acute to suggest the need for a socialism that can offer some real prospect of human community and solidarity. Beyond this, perhaps the clearest and most perilous indication of the conflict between the private rationality of market capitalism and a universal human rationality is in the sphere of the physical environment itself, where the necessity for an eco-socialism might be thought to be alarmingly apparent.

Yet the fact that capitalism remains vulnerable to the moral arguments and empirical theory of socialism, and that the need for a 'social' order to be imposed upon the operation of market capitalism can be shown to be more necessary than ever, does not by itself provide the grounds for optimism about the future prospects of socialism. The belief that it did provide such grounds has, of course, been a source of much false comfort for socialists in the past. If there is to be development in a socialist direction in the capitalist democracies of the West (where it makes much more sense to think of socialism as a process than as a product), then it seems sensible to believe that this will depend not merely upon the ability of capitalism to continue to generate moral and material dissatisfactions, but also, and even mainly, upon the ability of socialists to offer a convincing and credible alternative. It is significant that it is an insistent theme on the part of the defenders of capitalist democracy that, to coin a phrase, there is no alternative. Equally significantly, in the defence of capitalist democracy it has usually been the democracy and not the capitalism that is defended, in a conflation designed to suggest that one is inseparable from the other. As G. D. H. Cole remarked in the 1930s, this is capitalism's best card. Even though it loses much of its force once it is remembered that most political despotisms have existed in societies founded upon private property and that there are very different kinds of capitalist democracy, it still retains sufficient force to serve as a powerful ideological weapon.

An important reason why it is able to perform this function is that socialists have been able to argue only that it is *possible* to have socialist democracy, whereas capitalist democracy is not an argument but a fact (notwithstanding its evident imperfections). While both capitalism and socialism, as systems, have revealed themselves to be compatible with political despotism, only capitalism has revealed itself to be compatible with democracy and political freedom. This evidence has not gone unnoticed by the inhabitants of the capitalist democracies, including the working-class inhabitants, and has provided a powerful incentive to settle for what they have got, or at least for its social democratic version when they can get it. At the beginning of the twentieth century socialists assured the world that socialism was synonymous with human freedom, while anti-socialists warned that it was to be identified with coercion and tyranny. It can scarcely be claimed that the rest of the century has done much to strengthen the socialist side of the argument. Indeed, the voice of the capitalist anti-socialist was supplemented by the official voice of actually existing socialism in the denial of the viability of a democratic socialism. Both voices, of course, had a direct interest in sustaining this denial, and an equal amount to fear from its practical refutation.

What all this means is that the onus is now squarely on socialism. If it was once reasonable to take socialists, literally, at their word, this is no longer so. Many of their traditional words can be seen to have sustained positions that were thoroughly disingenuous, and people now rightly demand to see the colour of their money to check that they are not dealing in a debased currency. The character of the socialist alternative on offer in the capitalist democracies therefore becomes of central importance, and socialists face a considerable task of public persuasion. They will be disabled in this task if they do not take some trouble to acknowledge that there are demonstrably different kinds of socialism, both theoretically and practically, and go to further trouble to distinguish their own kind. There are many socialisms that have been in evidence around the world, and there are quite likely to be many more, in an assortment of ideological mixtures and capable of producing different amounts of benevolence and malevolence. Socialism, as the preceding account has endeavoured to illustrate, has always been multiform and not uniform, plural and not singular; and it is therefore both more honest and politically intelligent for socialists to shout this from the rooftops rather than to pretend that there is a 'real' socialism which exists and has existed nowhere but against which all actual socialisms are to be seen simply as a series of irrelevant and unfortunate historical mishaps.

A THIRD WAY?

It is not enough, then, for socialists to argue that western societies *need* socialism. They also have to be able to offer a kind of socialism that the citizens of these societies might be persuaded democratically to *want*. A socialism of this kind would need to be both attractive in principle and credible in practice. This would seem to imply a number of ingredients: first, a recognition that socialism is primarily (although not only) a moral theory, capable of generating a set of socialist values that can be articulated and applied in terms of a coherent public philosophy. In particular, this would involve a convincing account of a socialist conception of equality that genuinely enlarges freedom and autonomy, while also promoting community and fraternity. A socialism that takes its stand on this basis could not regard itself *solely* as the movement of a single class, or define itself *simply* in terms of the interests of a class, or define individuals *only* in terms of class categories, since this would be inconsistent with its general humanism. In so far as socialism aspires to represent a global humanism, an aspiration that is neither absurd nor irrelevant given the situation of the planet at the end of the twentieth century, there is a real sense in which its interests are everyone's interests. Not only is this true in principle, but it is reflected in the recent growth of significant movements (for example, the women's movement and the green movement) on the radical Left alongside and outside the traditional labour movement. If one kind of socialist responds to such developments by endeavouring to interpret and compress them within the traditional parameters of the labour movement, fortunately another kind learns from them that it is necessary to enlarge those parameters in the direction of a general movement of liberation. As Claus Offe has expressed it, 'the crucial problem for the labour movement is how to become *more* than a labour movement'.

However, a credible and attractive socialism would need to have some further ingredients. It would need to demonstrate its possession of a theory of political and economic organization that avoided mere statism. It would need to show that it knew how to abolish the capitalist form of the concentration of power and property without thereby inaugurating a new form of socialist concentration. In terms of the economy, this would clearly involve an accommodation between plan and market, in the interests of both efficiency and consumer choice, and with a range of forms of enterprise and social ownership but with a preference for the small-scale and the self-managing. It would need to combine dynamic markets with an intelligent state. In terms of the political system, it would involve the democratic diffusion of power in a system of explicit pluralism rooted in forms of territorial and functional devolution, in addition to effective general mechanisms to guarantee political accountability, representation and civic freedom. It would mean some kinds of power being exercised beyond the level of the nation state but other kinds of power being extended below. Whenever and wherever possible, consistent with general social and economic objectives, it would be an 'enabling' state, redistributing power and property in ways designed to strengthen and extend individual and group autonomy. Indeed, it seems increasingly plausible that general social and economic objectives will positively demand this sort of policy (in the direction of what André Gorz calls a 'dual society') in response to social and technological change. Utopia comes in from the cold.

Yet utopia also needs to have its feet on the ground. The kind of socialism described here has not merely to be selected from the political shelf, but rather to be constructed through political practice. If it is a kind of socialism that knows where it wants to go, it also has no illusions about the difficulties in getting there. While socialists certainly need good theory, they also have an urgent need for successful practice (and rather less 'praxis'). Ideas work through example, and many of the examples of socialism offered in this century have inflicted considerable damage on the idea. If the best argument for socialism in Britain has been the National Health Service, then the shadow of the Gulag has hung like a black cloud over the whole socialist project. Socialism badly needs more successes in developing new forms of ownership and enterprise and new kinds of collective individualism in a range of policy areas if people are to be convinced that it offers practical answers to the problems of the age. For similar reasons, socialist parties and organizations might reasonably be expected to prefigure in their internal life the sort of procedures and relationships they want to bring to the wider society. Parties that promise fraternity but practise fratricide (as with the Labour Party in Britain in the 1980s) deserve to have a credibility problem.

Finally, in looking back over the history of socialist ideas and movements, it is in the democratic socialist tradition that the materials for the kind of socialism described here are mainly to be found. In important respects this has been a minority tradition, squeezed for much of its life between an authoritarian communism and an unadventurous labourism. As a tradition it carries the considerable historical distinction of having added 'democratic' to socialism at a time when it mattered, to differentiate itself from an undemocratic socialism. However, it further distinguished itself by preferring to describe itself as democratic socialist in preference to social democratic, when this also came to matter. If social democrats are liberals who really mean it, then democratic socialists are social democrats who really mean it. It is a tradition that has been predominantly non-Marxist, but not necessarily anti-Marxist. A further dimension to its title derives from the fact that it has been the place where those socialists who have wanted not merely to defend but to extend democracy in new directions have found a home.

In many respects the loosening and eventual disappearance of the rival socialist blocs in recent decades has widened the constituency for this kind of democratic socialism, as part of a more general opening towards neglected and minority traditions, notwithstanding the fact that it has occurred in the immediate context of neo-liberal triumphalism. While this is much to be welcomed, it has in some respects made it more difficult to construct a viable and coherent democratic socialist political practice. In Britain, in particular, this was conspicuously the case for a period, when the Labour Party was immobilized by the combined effects of a vulgar labourism and a vulgar Marxism and unable to develop a democratic socialism that was both theoretically and practically credible in the face of the resurgent market liberalism with which it was confronted. This kind of democratic socialism or social democracy would represent a genuine third way between state socialism and irresponsible capitalism. It would also demand a considerable amount of political skill and practical imagination, from both its leaders and its supporters. It would involve a long haul, with many failures and mistakes on the way, and without any assurance of eventual success or lasting victory. It would have to live on its resources. In this sense, as Aneurin Bevan explained, it is profoundly misleading to describe it as a political middle way:

> Democratic Socialism is not a middle way between capitalism and Communism. If it were merely that, it would be doomed to failure from the start. It cannot live by borrowed vitality. Its driving power must derive from its own principles and the energy released by them. It is based on the conviction that free men can use free institutions to solve the social and economic problems of the day, if they are given the chance to do so.

8   A new socialism?

Once socialism is defined in this way – as social-ism – we can be liberated
from our history and not chained by it.

(Tony Blair)

But where does socialism stand now? Is there a new socialism to be
constructed out of the variety of socialisms discussed here? We know
where the socialist tradition has come from, but is it possible to see
where it might now be going? Before offering some concluding thoughts
on these large questions, it is useful to look a little more closely at the
British case. For it is in Britain that such questions are most clearly framed,
and where the answers given are likely to acquire a more general
significance.

THE BRITISH CASE

The focus here is on recent socialist thinking in Britain. By 'recent' is
meant the period since the end of the 1970s, the prolonged period when
the Labour Party was out of power. This situation forced the party –
and the Left generally – to take fundamental stock of its position and
condition. The result of this has been described as a 'new revisionism',
which, by the early 1990s, seemed to have had a remarkable effect in
restoring Labour's political fortunes and by the mid-1990s had produced a
'new' Labour with a new ideology. This gives a particular interest to the
British case in terms of the general fortunes of social democracy in recent
times; and the discussion here is concerned more with the development of
ideas on the left than with the internal processes of the Labour Party. On
the basis of the ideological evolution sketched here, some concluding
reflections are offered on its relevance to the wider world of social
democracy.

Living off the past

The defeat of the Labour Party in the election of 1979 was a defining moment in British politics. Labour had been in office for all but four of the preceding fifteen years and the Conservative Party had begun to ask questions about its own political future, moving sharply to the right and electing a new leader. Labour's 1979 defeat, the immediate product of economic difficulties and industrial strife, was therefore not merely an important political moment but also an important ideological moment. It brought not only Mrs Thatcher to power but also 'Thatcherism', that neo-liberal New Right cocktail of a 'free economy and strong state' (in Andrew Gamble's useful phrase). It also brought significant consequences for Labour and the Left. The Right set about attacking the postwar social democratic order which had provided Labour's working assumptions for so long. That order had already seemed to be breaking down in the late 1970s, taking Labour down with it in 1979 and providing an opening for the Right's brand of muscular capitalism freed from the excrescences of the social democratic state.

This development threw the Left into considerable confusion and disorientation. Labour gave every impression of being politically and intellectually exhausted. Even if it had won the 1979 election it is not clear that it would have known what to do with its victory. The postwar settlement seemed to have broken down, with its underpinnings of Keynes plus welfare state, but only the Thatcherites of the New Right appeared both to welcome this fact and to have a programme to offer in response. When its most basic assumptions were challenged in this way, Labour had lived off them for so long that it found it very difficult to respond to the challenge. It could raise the standard of 'anti-Thatcherism', but that was itself an acknowledgement that the Right had seized the initiative.

There was, in consequence, an urgent need for the British Left to undertake a programme of intellectual and political renewal, but the nature of the Labour Party made this a more difficult and problematic exercise than it should have been. There are a number of factors here, which can be touched on only briefly. Called upon to define what it stood for, in the conditions of the 1980s, Labour was unaccustomed to such a request and unsure how to respond. Indeed, there was even a doubt that it could make an effective response in view of its particular organizational and theoretical structure. Organizationally, it was a federal structure, rooted in a trade union basis, and this made the task of concerted and coherent policy-making always difficult. (As it was once memorably remarked of the task of Labour Party leadership: 'A leader who cannot ride two bloody horses at once has no right to a job in the bloody circus.') When the party's internal structures are pulling in different directions, as they were for much of the late 1970s and early 1980s, this makes effective leadership – and decisive policy-making – almost impossible.

However, the party's theoretical character is no less important. It is both an organizational and a theoretical hybrid, reflecting its turn-of-the-century foundation on an uneasy mixture of trade union interest and domestic socialist ideology. British socialism, an ethical utopianism stiffened with Fabian rationalism, was then regarded with theoretical contempt by the scientific Marxists of the Second International (although, as we saw earlier, Bernstein's 'revisionism' owed something to his association with British Fabianism). The infant Labour Party had, in 1918, adopted a socialist programme:

> to secure for the workers by hand or by brain the full fruits of their industry and the most equitable distribution thereof that may be possible upon the basis of the common ownership of the means of production, distribution and exchange, and the best obtainable system of popular administration and control of each industry or service.

However, this programmatic collectivism had to coexist with a pragmatic labourism which underpinned the party. This was the 'direct interests of labour', which the Labour Representation Committee (the precursor of the Labour Party at the beginning of the century) was formed to promote. It consisted of an untheoretical meliorism, the application of trade unionism to the wider world of party politics. Yet these different positions and perspectives did provide a suitably accommodating ideological umbrella under which all could comfortably shelter – from Marxists to social democrats, labourists to Christian utopians – and provided some useful ideological glue to hold together the assorted worshippers in what was often described as Labour's 'broad church'.

This last phrase is significant. Part of the distinctiveness of British Labour in a wider European context is its effective monopoly on the Left. This has been a considerable political asset, but a price has had to be paid for it. Part of that price has been a reluctance to engage in the sort of theoretical debates which might imperil the survival of its fragile internal coalition. Thus the party's socialist basis, as enshrined in that famous Clause IV (part IV) of the 1918 constitution, became an ancestral shrine to be worshipped, defended, and protected rather than one point in a continuing theoretical journey. The fact that its commitment to comprehensive collectivization of the economy was ever further removed from the party's political practice was not thought to be a problem requiring some theoretical attention (but, instead, to be a good reason for resolute inattention).

A group of 'revisionists' in the party did make a concerted attempt to address the issue in the 1950s and early 1960s, with Anthony Crosland's

The Future of Socialism (1956) standing as the representative text of the period. Crosland's insistence on 'the need for a restatement of doctrine' was based on an analysis of the changing circumstances with which modern socialists were faced:

> Traditional socialism was largely concerned with the evils of traditional capitalism, and with the need for its overthrow. But today traditional capitalism has been reformed and modified almost out of existence, and it is with a quite different form of society that socialists must now concern themselves.

The contemporary task was not to replace capitalist ownership with public ownership but to promote the fundamental socialist goal of social equality by new means. However when Gaitskell, as party leader, tried to persuade Labour formally to embrace this new ideological orientation, he not only failed to carry the party with him down the revisionist path but also provoked the kind of storm that warned against future ideological excursions of a similar kind.

Thus, the disjuncture between theory and practice remained, along with the belief that it was best to let sleeping ideological dogs lie. Therefore British Labour did not have its Bad Godesberg, much to the regret of Crosland, Gaitskell, and the revisionists. The result, though, was that Labour increasingly lived in a theoretical void, living off its past (with 1945 and the achievements of its postwar Government as its reference point) and content to settle for a pragmatic political practice (as in its embrace of 'modernization' as a unifying theme in the 1960s) personified by Harold Wilson and his governments of the 1960s and 1970s. When that political practice hit the rocks in the rough economic waters of the 1970s, Labour's traditional refusal to take seriously the task of defining what kind of party it was meant that it had little to fall back on beyond a solidaristic loyalty which was itself ever more precarious and conditional.

Finding a response

This background, briefly sketched, throws some light on Labour's difficulties in the 1980s. This period, with the party out of office and suffering repeated election defeats, was a challenge to it to undertake a process of revision and renewal. Yet it was precisely this which it found so difficult and had studiously avoided in the past. It required both an organizational and an intellectual response which it was singularly ill equipped to make.

One reflection of this was the way in which organizational and ideological questions became inextricably interwoven in the party in the 1980s, because both were at issue, both part of the problem and of any way forward. Indeed, ideological issues tended to be treated as if they were organizational issues (as in the party's response to the 'entryism' of the Trotskyite Militant Tendency), since the party's ideological coyness did not provide a secure basis for deciding which of the many varieties of 'socialists' were legitimate members of Labour's broad church. The impression of the 1980s, then, is of many of Labour's chickens coming home to roost – and causing quite a commotion in the farmyard.

The party was rudderless, without either secure doctrinal anchorage or organizational coherence. The party's social democratic wing was in retreat, shipwrecked by the economic storms and belt-tightening of the 1970s. The confident revisionism of two decades earlier, secure in a Keynesian social democracy of managed growth and extended welfare, had been undermined by the sheer force of events that confounded the analysis. The problems of capitalism had demonstrably not been solved and this left a merely distributional socialism confused and intellectually bereft. This is why, even if Labour had managed to win the 1979 general election, it would not have known what to do with its victory.

It is not surprising, therefore, that the initiative within Labour's ranks moved decisively leftwards, just as the Conservatives moved sharply to the right. Both left and right could agree that social democracy had failed and that a more muscular kind of ideological politics was required. On the left the response was both organizational and ideological. A series of reforms to Labour's constitution was engineered, designed to empower party activists at the expense of the parliamentary leadership (which was held responsible for the party's misfortunes); while an 'alternative' economic programme of planning and protection was embraced in place of a failed Keynesianism, along with a commitment to shed Britain's nuclear deterrent. The intellectual roots of this new position had been laid during the 1970s, in an analysis (the key text was Stuart Holland's *The Socialist Challenge*, 1975) that identified ownership and control of strategic companies within a framework of planning as the modern route to socialism. As Labour in office struggled, so the left's analysis gained ground and, after the party's defeat in 1979, came into its own. Yet it was a curious ideological mixture, sternly centralist in its belief in economic planning and the importance of ownership but also wanting to speak the language of workers' control and participatory democracy. The nature of this mixture, with all its tensions and incipient contradictions, was best revealed in the assorted thoughts of Tony Benn, its leading protagonist.

This was a period of intense turmoil and factionalism in the party, ideologically turbulent, personally bitter, and organizationally chaotic. The vacuum in the party had been filled, because vacuums have to be filled, by a leftward lurch engineered by party activists of assorted persuasions, a number of trade unions, and with Tony Benn (who came within a fraction of being elected deputy leader of the party in 1981 under the new rules) as its spearhead and spokesman. It was the period of 'socialism in one country'; but it was also the period when the party seemed to be tearing itself apart, even raising questions about its long-term survival. The verdict seemed likely to be either political suicide or death by immobilism.

Certainly the consequences were severe and immediate. A secession from the party in 1981 by a group of leading figures on the social democratic wing issued in the formation of the Social Democratic Party, which, in alliance with the Liberals, was to score some notable electoral successes during the following two years and thus help to ensure that a divided opposition made it easier for Mrs Thatcher's Conservatives to stay in power. The new party claimed, at least initially, to stand for a non-statist version of socialism in opposition to Labour's collectivism and corporatism, but the link with socialism was soon weakened in favour of the embrace of a 'social market' orientation. For a time it seemed that this might be the beginning of a realignment of the Left in Britain that had often been projected but never accomplished. Certainly the circumstances were propitious. The Labour Party had taken up position in a sectarian bunker somewhere to the left of the French Communist Party and this had opened up much unoccupied political territory. It seemed possible that Labour's monopoly on the left would be broken and British distinctiveness in this respect ended. The organizational and ideological coalition that was the Labour Party seemed finally to be coming apart.

This very nearly happened. Labour's turmoil brought it electoral disaster. In the 1983 election it was humiliated, reduced to its lowest level of support in its modern history and only marginally ahead of the alliance of Social Democrats and Liberals. It had nearly, only four years after being in government, managed to reduce itself to the status of a third party. This was a truly remarkable political achievement, especially in view of the un-popularity of the Thatcher Government for much of this period. The party was saved only by the dogged loyalty of its core support in a shrinking working-class base. Needing to reach out, it had pulled in, a phenomenon and a fate similar to the communist parties in Europe. In 1983 it had reached the edge of the electoral precipice and glimpsed the abyss below.

Having seen one possible future, it opted for an alternative, although this was not as straightforward as it sounds (for some of the reasons already discussed) and involved a protracted and painful period of recovery and reorientation, the fruits of which were not to be seen for a considerable time. Indeed, it was not until after a further election defeat, in 1987, that the task of reconstruction was taken seriously in hand. Until then, in the mid-1980s, Labour had remained in political limbo. With a new leader, Neil Kinnock, it had begun to distance itself from the shambles of the early 1980s and improved its presentation and organization, but it remained at the mercy of events, had made policy compromises rather than policy choices, and still lacked a clear identity and direction. After its third consecutive election defeat in 1987, though, the party leadership embarked on a fundamental and comprehensive policy review. This sought to link the themes of social justice and economic efficiency, and to combine a recognition of the central role of markets with the activity of what was now called an 'enabling' state.

This policy review was accompanied by a statement of the party's *Aims and Values*, presented as a general statement about democratic socialism, the need for which was a recognition that in the ideological politics of the 1980s the offensive had come from the Right and required a response from the Left. However, this response – seen more fully in a book (*Choose Freedom*, 1987) by Roy Hattersley, the party's deputy leader – was more a recapitulation of old truths, especially on the theme that real freedom was enhanced not diminished by socialism, contrary to the claims of the New Right, than an attempt to break new theoretical ground. Nor was it intended to supplant the sacred cow of the 1918 constitution as a statement of Labour's fundamental purpose.

Yet the fact remains that this sustained episode of policy revision, culminating in the approval of the policy review documents at the party's 1989 conference, was an extraordinary political achievement. It was a story, as one account put it, of Labour Rebuilt. It had been a revolution from above, perhaps the only way in which it could have been accomplished given Labour's disparate structure, and owing much to the formidable political skills and courage of the Kinnock leadership. Even then, there had been those who had doubted whether it was possible, simply because of the scale of the task and Labour's essentially centrifugal character. On this view, what was remarkable was not that Labour needed to respond to its electoral plight and internal disintegration, but that an effective response was so long in coming. When it did come, it continued to reflect that mixture of organizational and doctrinal issues noticed earlier, designed now to empower the party's members at the expense of its activists and to create a more effective and representative organizational structure. As ever, organizational, doctrinal, and policy matters were closely interwoven.

In crude political terms, Labour had signalled a shift away from the leftism of the early 1980s and towards the progressive centre. In an important sense, the party's policy review was significant less for what it contained than for what it symbolized. Luck also came to the party's aid too. The alliance of Social Democrats and Liberals fell apart, thereby giving Labour a new opening to the centre. Then Gorbachev helped to dig Labour out of the black hole of its non-nuclear defence policy. Symbolism apart, though, Labour's policy shift did reflect a wider debate on the Left during the 1980s about the problems and possibilities of socialism in the contemporary situation. Aspects of this debate illuminate some of the larger questions about socialism asked earlier.

A new revisionism

The mood of this debate was pessimistic, though sometimes buoyantly so. This was understandable, since the problem to be addressed was the historically unexpected renewal of the market capitalist Right and the associated decline of the Left. Indeed the underlying question, asked at interminable 'Whither Socialism?' seminars, was whether there was any longer a political future for the Left at all. The iconoclastic arrogance of the early 1980s had dissolved into a deep uncertainty. That earlier flirtation with one-country socialism behind protective walls now looked absurd in face of the late-twentieth-century global economy (and the collapse of the Mitterrand experiment in France), but it was not clear what should be embraced instead. A failed corporatism in the 1970s, in the face of both accelerating unemployment and high inflation, had seemed to mark the end of any option of returning to social democratic Keynesianism as a method of addressing the structural problems of the British economy. The mood of the times seemed to be for less state, not more, while the need for public spending cuts – along with tax resistance on the part of the electorate – also undermined a traditional part of the Left's welfare programme. Many of these issues adversely affected the fortunes of social democratic parties in Europe, but in Britain – both because of its particular economic problems and the particular disabilities of the Labour Party – their impact was especially severe.

However, the malaise and uncertainty on the left went even deeper than this. The real question, and anxiety, was whether the Left in general, and Labour in particular, was a movement in historical retreat, the product of yesterday but with nothing to say about tomorrow. Not merely with nothing to say, but with a declining base and constituency. As long ago as 1978, the communist historian Eric Hobsbawm had asked whether, in view of changes in the industrial and occupational class structure, the historical advance of the labour movement should be seen as having 'halted' and, if so, what consequences and lessons there might be for the politics of labour. The question provoked much controversy and debate, both at the time and subsequently, and was generalized into larger questions of constituency, identity and strategy. Some wanted to defend the viability of a traditional class politics rooted in the trade unions; others sought to argue that the 'new social movements' provided the basis for a rainbow coalition of the dispossessed. Still others, including Hobsbawm himself (whose views were said to be influential with Labour leader Kinnock), argued that Labour had to become a people's party in a context where the urgent strategic need was to build a progressive anti-Thatcher coalition.

This strategic, and tactical, debate was an important strand in the politics of the Left in the 1980s, but it was grounded in the larger question of the character of the 'new times' in society, economy, culture, and politics (a question explored at length by the journal *Marxism Today*), with answers – as far as the future of the Left was concerned – which were at best uncertain and at worst positively gloomy. There was a nice inversion of Marx at work here: the point, it almost seemed, was not to change the world but to interpret it. This world was judged to be post-Fordist, post-modernist, post-everything; with all the traditional supports of a left-wing politics rooted in the labour movement in erosion and decline. Organized mass production had produced an organized working class which could be organized by left-wing parties and labour movements on national lines, but now all the elements in this scenario were being subverted by new processes of disaggregation and diversification. Did this mean that 'new times' belonged to the New Right? Should 'post-socialist' be added to the lexicography of the age? Or could the Left find a new identity, programme, and constituency appropriate to the times?

It was this last question, widely asked but without clear answer, which underpinned the policy revisions and ideological adjustments of this period. To label this the 'new revisionism' is to suggest that it all had an organizing coherence, which is really not so, but a number of significant themes may be identified. There was, for example, an attempt to disengage socialism from its identification with the state and statism. This had a number of aspects. It was reflected conceptually in the idea of an 'enabling' or 'empowering' state, an idea which gained much currency. Here the state opened the way for individuals and groups to pursue their own purposes rather than simply adhere to its own. It was possible to present this as a new kind of socialist individualism, certainly of a socialism which took individual rights and empowerment as its central theme and sought to trump the Right in its embrace of the extended rights of individuals. Indeed, there was a remarkable revival on the left of the idea of citizenship, as an organizing concept capable of renewing arguments about the nature of civil and political rights in Britain but also extending the argument into the arena of social and economic rights. There was, likewise, a widespread identification of civil society as the key site of the new politics.

This emphasis, away from central statism and towards new approaches, was reflected in the way in which socialists now tackled assorted policy areas. For example, discussions of welfare were less in terms of a traditional welfare statism, criticized by the Left no less than the Right for its top-down bureaucracy, and more in terms of finding new forms of service delivery which were user-friendly and concerned with issues of quality. More generally, there was an emphasis on decentralization as a response to the centralized nature of the British state and to some of the traditional defects of British public administration. Crucially, too, in thinking about economic and industrial policy there was a shift away from dirigism and towards a more market-oriented approach. At a theoretical level, there was a renewal of interest in models of market socialism on the Left; while at a policy level there was a general rejection of nationalization (even of most of the newly privatized industries) in favour of regulatory models and schemes for wider share-ownership. Planning, that traditional economic prescription on the left, was out of favour, at least in terms of macro-economic management; instead there was the micro-economic emphasis of 'supply-side socialism' with its attention to structural and sectoral improvements.

In other areas, too, new thinking and themes were apparent on the left. One of the striking, and perhaps most enduringly significant, developments of the late 1980s was the embrace of Europe by the British Left, after many years of insular suspicion. Politics was European and, beyond that, global. In thinking about the economy, or the environment (the salience of which also increased sharply for the Left in this period), the context and terrain was inescapably international. Other issues also made their appearance on the left in the 1980s, one of which deserves particular mention. This was an increased dissatisfaction, fired by the authoritarianism of the Thatcher years, with the quality of British democracy and the nature of the British constitution. In general terms, the Left had always been constitutionally complacent and conservative, but now a movement (Charter 88) was launched on the Left to campaign for the comprehensive reconstruction of the British constitution (involving a Bill of Rights, a constitutional document and electoral reform). Again this may turn out to be one of the more unexpected, and most significant, legacies of the politics of the 1980s.

All this is shorthand, and describes a general climate of ideas rather than specific policy positions. However, the two were closely related, as the Labour Party's key policy review document *Meet the Challenge, Make the Change* (1989) clearly revealed. The party had not only dropped certain policies which had come to be seen as electoral liabilities (such as unilateral nuclear disarmament), but had also adjusted to the new climate. It had clearly embraced the market. It had sought to shed its producerist image, rooted in its trade union basis, and embraced consumers and consumerism. It had also responded to its identification with distributional issues by emphasizing its commitment to production (caring was not enough, unless you could pay for it) and competent economic management. It had even signalled its support for a series of constitutional reforms, though still stopping short of the constitutional revolution advocated by the radical reform movement.

In all of this it had sought to present the Thatcherite Right as the ideological extremists, increasingly out of step with the times and with the European mainstream, and to present itself as the carrier of a new ideological consensus of social and industrial partnership. Yet it remained an uncertain response to the times, reactive and defensive, a necessary adjustment in the face of a hostile environment rather than a positive and confident process of theoretical and political renewal. There was a sense that old models had ceased to work, but without a secure grasp of any developed alternatives. Discrete policy initiatives were plentiful and designed to reposition Labour in significant ways, but this process was not accompanied by a larger and more fundamental enterprise of doctrinal reconstruction. It was probably as far as the party could go, farther than many wanted it to go, yet it nevertheless left it between two worlds and with basic issues of identity and belief unresolved.

Although it is not of direct concern here, the relationship between the general debate on the left and the policy review process in the Labour Party deserves mention. Labour's review process had been very much an internal affair, feeding off and reflecting the larger debates but not really engaging with them. The party had not sought to initiate any serious theoretical debate, unlike parties of the left elsewhere in this period, although certain party figures did produce texts on the new revisionism (such as Bryan Gould's *A Future for Socialism*, 1989). The real debate went on elsewhere, in journals like *Marxism Today* and *New Statesman*, in interventions by academics in groups such as the Socialist Philosophy Group within the Fabian Society (where market socialist ideas were revived) and initiatives such as the newsletter *Samizdat* with its advocacy of a centre-left 'popular front of the mind'. These were not party initiatives (although at the end of the 1980s a new quasi-party think tank, the Institute of Public Policy Research, was established to mirror the plethora of right-wing think tanks which had nourished the rise of Thatcherism a decade earlier). Perhaps all this simply reflects the character of the Labour Party referred to earlier, or even the wider British political tradition. Ideas are dangerous things, and intellectuals even more so. Both are best avoided if at all possible.

Whatever the process, though, the political result was striking. The revival of the political fortunes of the Labour Party from the nadir of the early 1980s was dramatic, while the climate of ideas also became more favourable to the Left. Indeed, it is worth remarking that survey research consistently revealed a strong attachment to collectivist values in Britain through much of the 1980s, despite the political ascendancy of Thatcherism.

These values seemed to be strengthened further as the 1980s turned into the 1990s, perhaps reflecting a disenchantment with purely market solutions and a concern with the condition of public services. Some even suggested that the Me years were giving way to the We years. The Labour Party, armed with its new policies and new image, was the clear beneficiary of this development. It even began to seem possible, despite requiring an electoral shift greater than at any period since 1945, that Labour might again form a government when the election came in 1992.

However, there were still those who raised questions about Labour's renaissance. A running question, first asked by a leading political commentator, was whether the party had yet discovered a Big Idea. Was its pragmatic revisionism enough? There were lots of new ideas, but was there a New Idea capable of giving coherence to assorted policy initiatives and a contemporary identity to the Left? Was Labour engaged in fundamental ideological renewal, or merely tactical policy adjustment? Was its shift to be seen as radical, or conservative? Had it, anyway, gone down the individualist road at the very moment when the tide of opinion had seemingly begun to move sharply in a communitarian direction? These were some of the questions on the table for Labour at the beginning of the 1990s. However, they were very different questions from those which had been asked about it – concerning its own survival and the future of its ideas – only a few years previously.

Or so it was believed, until the party's fourth consecutive election defeat in 1992 once again forced a return to the drawing board. Now the battle was joined between those who believed that some further pragmatic adjustment of policy and position would eventually restore the party's electoral fortunes and those who believed that a fundamental engagement with the party's identity and beliefs could no longer be avoided. The election of Tony Blair as party leader in 1994, following the sudden death of John Smith, ensured that the latter course would be adopted. The task was nothing less than the creation of a new party – and this required a new ideological basis. The replacement of the old Clause IV with a new statement of democratic socialist values meant that, in 1995, Labour did finally have its Bad Godesberg. Moreover, the battle of ideas was now not only central to the party but driven from the top. The Blairite revolution, converting socialism into 'social-ism' and constructing a liberal communitarianism anchored in a broad intellectual inheritance of the left centre, succeeded where the putative revisionism of a generation earlier had failed. The means and ends of socialism had finally been disentangled, not through evasion or obfuscation but through a direct and explicit process of theoretical reconstruction. On any test it was a decisive and defining moment for the

British Left, both politically and intellectually, with a significance for socialism that went wider still.

If this story has an interim conclusion, it is that the British Labour Party has finally become a European social democratic party. At the beginning of the 1980s it seemed closer to the communist parties of Europe, and experienced a similar political fate. Both doctrinally and organizationally, British Labour has now decided what kind of party it wants to be and has set about becoming such a party. Its ability to reinvent itself will depend on whether it can construct a new political space between the older failures of postwar Keynesian social democracy and the newer failures of the neo-liberal counter-revolution. Its future and its fate will be the future and fate of the democratic Left in Europe as a whole.

TOWARDS A NEW SOCIALISM

But what will that future and fate be? Has not British Labour renewed itself in a social democratic direction when social democracy is everywhere in crisis and disarray? Is it really possible to forge a 'new' socialism out of such unpromising materials and in such an inhospitable environment? The short answer is that we do not know. The longer answer is that we would be foolish not to try. What follows is a brief attempt to explain why.

Where we are now

There can be no refuge in the bogus optimism provided by old doctrinal baggage. The economic theory of socialism, that social ownership is a more efficient general way of organizing production than capitalist markets, is dead. So too are the scientism and historicism that allowed socialists (of assorted persuasions) to believe that they had cracked the historical code and discovered the laws of social dynamics. Gone also is the assumed link between socialism and its traditional social agent in the working class. With so much that was long thought to be central to socialism gone, is there really anything of substance left?

What is left is what is most essential to socialism, even if some socialists have not always recognized this in their preoccupation with the inessentials. For what is left is what socialism is, an ethic of community and mutual responsibility, a way of thinking about the proper relationship of individuals to each other and to society at large. There are other ways of thinking about these things, but this is the socialist way. In so far as politics is an arena of moral choice, this is the choice that socialists elect to make. In so far as choices carry consequences with them, socialists believe that the social consequences that flow from their choice are to be preferred to those that flow from other choices. This does not mean that an easy policy manual comes attached, nor that the cluster of values that contribute to the socialist ethic are always in effortless symmetry, nor that socialism stands wholly apart from other traditions with which it shares a common inheritance; but it does mean a particular view of what a community is and what, through common endeavour and cooperative purpose, it may be able to achieve.

All this may seem loftily removed from the actual circumstances in which socialists now find themselves. If the twentieth century has witnessed a systemic struggle between capitalism and socialism, it looked by the middle of the century (even to those – such as Schumpeter and Hayek – who wished for a different outcome) as if socialism had gained the decisive upper hand. The French socialist leader Léon Blum struck a representative note at the end of the Second World War when he described socialism as having arrived at its 'triumphant period' when

> Socialist assumptions and axioms have been taken over by men and parties who have waged the most ferocious of wars against socialist organisations. It is on the foundation of socialist principles that societies, whether consciously or not, are everywhere being reconstituted.

Yet here we are at the end of the century with a very different kind of triumphalism in evidence. The battle seems finally to be over and capitalist principles to have won. The postwar social democratic compromise has come unstuck as market liberalism has reasserted itself, while the command economies that presented the only functioning alternative to capitalism have collapsed. The nature of that alternative had succeeded in making even the word 'social' a term of deep suspicion among those who had liberated themselves from it. As for socialism, Hilary Wainwright was told by a young Czech activist she met after the 'velvet' revolution that such was its weight of contamination that 'the word acts as an interruption in our conversation'. Moreover the contamination had served to infect perceptions of the socialist project in places far away from its source.

This is the context for the bout of 'endism' (of history, of socialism, of all alternatives to liberalism and capitalism) that has characterized the final decade of the twentieth century in the realm of social thought. If this kind of analysis is eminently plausible, it is also manifestly inadequate. In part this is because it falls into the oldest of theoretical traps that involves, as Orwell once characterized it, believing that the future will simply be an extension of tendencies to be found in the present. But, more significantly, these tendencies are themselves more complex and contested than a simple triumphalism allows. There are questions to be asked about the nature of those nominated both as victors and as vanquished. The victory may be claimed by the market militants of the neo-liberal right, but it was not their kind of capitalism that was put into battle against socialism and communism when it really mattered. David Marquand makes the point well:

> It was the capitalism of the long post-war boom, the capitalism of *Mitbestimmung* and the *Commissariat Général du Plan*, the capitalism of the paid holidays, the tight labour markets and the rising welfare expenditures that won the race with the regimes of eastern Europe, not the capitalism of the Great Depression. If the contest had been between Herbert Hoover and the command economy, the command economy might have won.

But it was not just against communism that a reformed capitalism was decisive, for it also offered itself as the basis for a historic compromise with socialism in the West – a compromise which many socialists were disposed to accept. In fact, an earlier announcement that ideology had ended was made on precisely this basis. If some socialists were foolish enough then not to understand that such a compromise was worth having, so the market triumphalists are foolish enough now to try to pass off an earlier and different victory as their own.

There is a similar point to be made about the post-communist societies of Eastern and Central Europe. For what was embraced, as communism was rejected was not the unreconstructed capitalism of the first half of the twentieth century but the prospect of a share in the reformed capitalism that had become the western hallmark in the second half of the century. As J. K. Galbraith puts it,

> Those who speak, as so many do so glibly, even mindlessly, of a return to the Smithian free market are wrong to the point of a mental vacuity of clinical proportions. It is something we in the West do not have, would not tolerate, could not survive. Ours is a mellow, government-protected life; for Eastern Europeans, pure and vigorous capitalism would be no more welcome than it would be for us.

The first free elections in these countries had been a referendum on communism. Subsequent elections have already made it abundantly clear that this was not to be the last word on the nature of the preferred alternative.

This book has been an exploration of the theme that there are different kinds of socialism. But there are different kinds of capitalism too; and it is clearer now than it has been in the past that the choice is not between systemic alternatives but different kinds of accommodation. To some this will seem less heroic and inspiring than in socialism's glory days. It may not even be how choices will present themselves in fifty or a hundred years' time, when some of today's imaginative utopias may have converted themselves into concretely available and pressingly urgent propositions. But it is our choice, now. It is also a tough choice, far tougher than when socialism and socialists could sustain themselves with the easy rhetoric of political messianism, and demanding a principled intelligence of a high order. The principle requires a clear identification of basic socialist values (which is why this enterprise in the Labour Party was so important); the intelligence is required for the application of these values in the world as it is. In this sense socialists need always to be both fundamentalists and revisionists, combining a firm anchorage of unchanging values with an ever-changing sense of how these values can get a purchase on the world. In the nice phrase of the Swedish socialist Wigforss, social democratic politics are always about a 'provisional utopia'.

The question now is about the kind of accommodation that is at issue. It goes beyond the limited 'mixed' economy, of the spheres of private and public enterprise, that once framed the question. It is asked in a context in which the market claims ever more for itself and the traditional supports of social democratic politics are badly eroded. A previous generation of socialist revisionism argued that an obsolete socialism of public ownership should be replaced by a new socialism of fiscal redistribution and social policy; but a newer socialism runs up against the resistance of a more differentiated society and is much less sure that even the tools of an older revisionism will work. The need for new thinking is evident. But of what kind? Is there a basis for a new political accommodation? Without doing more than entering a few thoughts in the register, it is nevertheless possible to sketch a general direction of advance.

A liberal socialism

This involves some clear thinking about the role of states and markets. If there is one lesson that socialists (and everybody else for that matter) should have learnt from the experience of the twentieth century it is that both states and markets have disabilities and that it is necessary to attend to both. Markets have all the dynamic merits that make them the most expedient way of organizing economic life; but they sometimes want to go where they should not, have an intrinsic and irresponsible blindness to the outcomes of their operation, and often have to be saved from themselves in the public interest. States properly represent the public interest; but they can develop private interests of their own (producer capture is not simply an invention of the Right), have tendencies that range from the inflexibly bureaucratic to the blatantly oppressive, and require a battery of devices to keep them on the straight and narrow. The Left's critique of the market is indispensible; but so is the Right's critique of the state. Moreover, as Michael Walzer argues, both states and markets can be totalitarian if they invade territory that is not their own. Thus both states and markets require regulation in the public interest.

This requires socialists to take more interest in the operation and organization of the state than they have generally displayed in the past. For example, it might be expected that those who are most committed to the public provision of services would also be those who display a restless ingenuity in ensuring that such provision is effective in terms of performance and outcome; yet this has often not been the case. It will have to be in future, if electorates are to be persuaded that public provision is worth paying for. There will also need to be new mechanisms for user involvement and control in public services. Moreover, this is likely to be in a context in which state and market, public and private, do not live in separate realms but inhabit a mix-and-match policy universe which is very different from the traditional model of a mixed economy. This means a clever state and intelligent markets. Market mechanisms may prove useful in certain areas of state activity (as long as it is remembered that the market makes a useful servant but a lousy master), while the state may perform an important role in making markets work better than they would do otherwise (sometimes dramatically so, as in the developmental states of East Asia). In the British case, Will Hutton has recently made a compelling case for the role of a clever state in remedying the structural infirmities of British capitalism. It is where a kind of socialism meets a kind of capitalism that the most interesting political territory is now to be found.

This is where the basis for a new consensus could be envisaged. Some will want to describe this as a 'social market' position, in so far as it seeks to combine a market economy with social responsibility. Yet the term is inadequate, for it puts adjective and noun in the wrong order. The market is an instrument; it is not a purpose. Only those who reject, or have forgotten, the idea of public purpose will accept such a reversal. It is like describing a cathedral in terms of the number of stones used in its construction. The language of 'market socialism' and 'liberal communitarianism' at least gets the order right. Yet there is a term with an older pedigree that best expresses what is intended: liberal socialism. This combines, in the proper relationship, the traditions that have defined and shaped progressive politics in the modern world. It qualifies socialism, as a doctrine of community and responsibility, with a liberal reminder of the dangers of an overweening state and the importance of individuals pusuing their own purposes in their own way. In its fusion – of state and market, public and private, common purpose and individual purpose – it opens up a whole policy agenda.

It provides the basis for a new kind of collectivism, which rescues the idea of collective action for social purposes from its identification with an old statism. Institutions, both public and private, can be redesigned to strengthen social responsibilities and develop active stakeholding. New forms of ownership can be nourished between state and market (if the old public utilities had been put on a mutual or cooperative basis their fate would have been very different) and new types of public interest company established. Social and welfare policy needs to combine a principle of inclusiveness, in the interests of equity and social integration, with opportunities for diversity and differentiation. A collective individualism uses public policy in imaginative ways to enable individuals to achieve their own purposes. Rights are extended, but so are responsibilities. A democracy of consumers is nourished, but so is a democracy of citizens. A rich pluralism of associational life is harnessed for the performance of tasks that elude remote states and atomized individuals alike. Democracy moves upwards to meet the demands of a new globalism, but it also moves downwards and sideways to sustain a new localism and new associationalism. An old collectivism may be dead, but a new collectivism is waiting to be born.

This does not mean that it will be. The future is unknown and unknowable. It may be better than the present, or worse. Much will depend upon the ability of democratic politics to provide a means whereby troubled citizens can make collective choices about public purposes and find the resilience to carry them through over a sustained period. Yet we are living at a time when the whole enterprise of collective democratic choice has been disparaged by the neo-liberal right. Only markets, a generation has been told, can frame choices, with the state reduced to the role of preserving the conditions within which market choice can operate (perhaps with a grudging additional nod in the direction of certain 'public goods' that the market is unable to provide). This language of choice can easily obscure the reality of power. The question is whether the democratic choice that citizens can make through politics is any match for the power that defines choice in terms of markets. In one guise the market is simply a mechanism, but in a more formidable guise it is the carrier of powers and interests. It is not surprising that democracy-as-choice is denigrated by the purveyors of market-as-choice, since the former represents the only challenger to the latter.

Beyond market individualism

If a liberal socialism requires an old collectivism to become a new collectivism (the failure to meet this requirement has played no small part in the recent problems of social democratic politics), an even more pressing precondition is that the contemporary tyranny of market individualism should be ended. Until this is accomplished, the basis for a new intellectual and political consensus simply will not exist. Already there are indications that this may be happening. A new language of community speaks to the times more convincingly than the abrasive othodoxies of possessive individualism. The fractured and fragmented condition of western societies cries out for a new politics of security and solidarity. Societies that are coming apart at the seams demand a principled reconstruction around common purposes, not a celebration of their disintegration at the hands of the careless gods of the market.

The straws in the intellectual wind begin to tell the same story. Communitarianism, both high and low, turns mood into theory. Fukuyama's celebrated discovery of the end of history is succeeded by his more anxious search for a new basis for social trust. The market liberals of the new conservatism are now to be seen trying desperately to conceal their nakedness with some remembered civic clothes. Even Robert Skidelsky's recent post-communist market manifesto, with its call for a dramatic reduction in public spending as a share of national income, incorporates the political health warning that 'the failures of collectivism everywhere led to the mistaken view that the state could do almost nothing and the market almost everything'. As that mistaken view converted itself into the conventional wisdom of the age, from which we are perhaps only now beginning to break free, it is important that its central errors should be fully understood. If state and market are to find a new synthesis, its terms and basis should not be in doubt.

There is a striking similarity between the kind of 'scientific' socialism discussed earlier and the creed of the new market ideologues. The fatal conceit of both is to describe their beliefs in terms of the operation of irresistible laws. Enough has already been said about socialism in this respect; but what is remarkable is the mirror-image to Marxism of the 'scientific' capitalism that conscripts history to its side and presents the global market as a kind of natural law with imperatives that peoples, states and societies are powerless to withstand. It is a measure of the extent to which purposive public action has been devalued that it is possible to think in this way. Nor is it entirely fanciful to see a further similarity between the Leninist cadres bringing, from without, the truths of scientific socialism to those who could not grasp them on their own and those shock therapists of capitalism whose mission it has been to instruct the post-communist societies of Eastern and Central Europe in the immutable laws of the market.

It is also curious that the market liberals of the New Right have been allowed to claim an intellectual victory. In fact, an intellectual project that involves the state doing less and markets doing more is sublimely straightfoward. It may be difficult politically (as the post-1979 experience of Britain has showed, where the state as taxer and spender expanded in the hands of those whose central ideological mission was to contract it), but it is not difficult intellectually. Selling off public industries (especially when public monopolies are simply converted into private ones), cutting taxes, reducing spending, and curtailing services in pursuit of an ideological objective is a programme fraught with political obstacles and dangers; but it is scarcely a programme for intellectual titans. Its thrust is essentially negative and destructive, a mission to dismantle rather than a project to construct. It requires only the sort of narrowly doctrinaire disposition associated in the past with a certain kind of socialist, coupled with a cheerful disregard for the consequences of what is essayed. When the consequences mock the prospectus, this is interpreted as the need for more strenuous efforts in the same direction instead of as an obligation to review the credentials of the prospectus itself.

The credentials are spurious, which is why a slavish adherence to market individualism has to be broken before a new politics can be constructed. As even wise conservatives have recognized, the neo-liberalism of the New Right is not merely too thin as a general account of social relations and obligations but, in unleashing the forces of market imperialism, it subverts the basis of community and legitimacy upon which a successful market society itself depends. In John Gray's words, 'the subversive effects of unhampered market institutions on traditional forms of life makes free-market conservatism an inherently unstable and, over time, a self-undermining political project'. It is scarcely surprising, therefore, that the evacuation by this kind of neo-liberal conservatism of much traditional conservative territory has invited its occupation by those socialists who take seriously the conditions for a common life. They may arrive from a different direction and bring their own view of what the conditions for a common life are, but they share with wise conservatives an understanding that a settled community cannot be founded upon the corrosive insecurities and dislocations unleashed by a doctrinaire politics of unbridled markets.

A new politics of liberal socialism will therefore be neither an old collectivism nor a new marketism. It will be diverse, pluralistic, and variegated, both politically and economically. It will be egalitarian enough to be socially inclusive, so that all its citizens are within reach of each other, but this will not be confused with identity of treatment or uniformity of provision. It will combine a commitment to a dynamic economy with a commitment to a decent society (it will hope, may even rhetorically assert, that the latter is a condition of the former, but its honest commitment is to both). It will know that its economic task is to make capitalism work more successfully, but it will also know that there are different kinds of capitalism. It will understand the virtues of markets, but also the vices. It will know that states can do too much, but also too little. It will recognize that decent societies pay decent taxes, but also that spending more on one thing usually means spending less on something else. It will celebrate diversity, but also seek to nourish social unity. In rejecting a whole range of false opposites, the space is opened for a new politics of liberal socialism to be endlessly inventive in exploring how a clever state can operate. Old collectivists and new marketeers will not like it, but that is another argument in its favour. If it is further and fashionably objected by the new globalists, whether of left or right, that single-country constructs are now irrelevant, at least part of the answer is that what is described here has its roots in the best of the European tradition (of social democracy, but also of christian democracy) and that it stands available for wider projects. The other part of the answer is that we have to start somewhere.

The relevance of socialism

So far, so revisionist. But it also requires a substantial dose of socialist fundamentalism. If liberal socialism offers a new synthesis, fertilized by different traditions, this should not obscure what is distinctive about the socialist contribution to it. This returns the discussion to the essentials of socialism, as an ethic of community and mutual responsibility, and to the relevance of that ethic now. What this means, in the simplest terms, is that we are all in it together, that society is not to be understood (either morally or empirically) as merely a maelstrom of atomized individuals but as a moral community embedded in a dense fabric of social relationships and obligations and capable of framing common purposes. There is nothing monolithic, oppressive, or nostalgic about this. Purposes, moralities, and communities are vigorously pluralistic; but this is merely the setting within which common understandings can be freely negotiated and translated into public policy (and such policy will always work best when it finds a congruence between individual purposes and wider public purposes). This approach contrasts both with a certain kind of old collectivism which sometimes seemed to want to impose its own purposes from above (emphatically so, of course, in the case of communism) and with a market philosophy which abstracts individuals from their social setting and denies that there can be any purposes other than individual ones.

At a time when even the idea of public purpose, and of purposive public action, has been so devalued and disparaged, socialism therefore retrieves and resurrects it. Free citizens can use the resources of a liberal and pluralistic democracy (resources which can and should be developed much further) to define their common purposes. Nor is it absurd, as some clever and many silly people suggest, to believe that a public interest can and should be constructed through the activity of democratic politics from the welter of particular and competing interests that bear down on every issue from all directions. This task should lie at the heart of political responsibility. It would not be neccessary to repeat such old and obvious truths if they had not been so recently and ferociously shunted off into the political sidings by the loose engines of market individualism. The implementation of common purposes will properly take place through the array of devices described earlier; but innovation on that front – between state and market, public and private – should not be confused with an improper repudiation of the idea of public purpose itself.

There are some further old truths too, central to the community ethic of socialism, that are in urgent need of recovery and restatement. It is as absurd to believe that freedom is necessarily enhanced when the state intervenes as it is to believe that freedom is necessarily diminished. If some socialists have had to unlearn the former belief, the purveyors of market freedom now have to be disabused (again) of the latter. It is extraordinary that an old liberal doctrine that was demolished so comprehensively by the 'new' liberalism of the early part of the twentieth century should have been allowed to find a new lease of life in the conservative neo-liberalism of the latter part of the century. The idea that most individuals become more free to the extent that the state recedes from their lives is preposterous, which does not prevent it being advanced with a straight face by people who should know better. If the community-as-state acts to prevent my environment being polluted or to ensure that I am treated when I am sick, then these are demonstrable gains in my freedom and not losses. This does not mean of course that all extensions of the role of the state are *ipso facto* gains for freedom. It is not neccessary to embrace that absurdity to repudiate its opposite; but it is the opposite that has come to represent the present danger.

Here another old socialist truth enters the picture. For what a belief in community entails is an understanding that many of our individual purposes can only be realized through acting together. That is at the heart of what collectivism is, once stripped of its tired statist associations. Some of our most pressing individual interests – in safe streets, clean air, training for jobs, education for our children, health care for our elderly parents and much else – can be achieved only through making collective provision with others for what we are not able to provide on our own. This does not mean that the state has to be the only provider, nor that a mixed economy of provision is not appropriate, nor that the state should not operate in new ways; but it does mean that the state is an indispensible (and often the most effective) provider of such services. Collective provision thus makes individual sense. Socialism should enable us to achieve collectively what we cannot achieve individually. Collective individualism is not a paradoxical phrase but a plain fact.

The opposition between 'state' and 'individual' so beloved by the neo-liberal Right turns out to be a chimera in crucial respects. In part this is because it leaves out all that lies between. For what lies between is what makes the world go round, the whole weight of powers and interests, groups and associations, that bears down on individuals and states alike. The market is the carrier of such powers and interests. If the public power of the state, as the official monopolist of legitimate force in society, needs vigilant scrutiny, so too does the private power of this unofficial world. It sometimes has to be saved from itself, and from us. The private rationality of market actors (such as dumping their 'externalities' on other people by polluting rivers, free-riding on training, or preferencing short-term rewards over long-term investments) can have a deep irrationality in public (and often private) terms. But the main point is that most individuals, when freed from the public power of the state, do not thereby come to inhabit a pure realm of self-government but live in a world in which private power of assorted kinds holds sway. Indeed, to the extent that private power drives out public power in a whole range of areas it becomes more, not less, difficult for individuals to advance their own interests and pursue their own purposes. The retreat from collective action in turn drives many people, not by the glories of choice but by the invisible hand of necessity, to seek private solutions to public problems. Brian Barry describes this unchosen process well:

> Does the public health service have long waiting lists and inadequate facilities? Buy private insurance. Has public transport broken down? Buy a car for each member of the family above driving age. Has the countryside been built over or the footpaths eradicated? Buy some elaborate exercise machinery and work out at home. Is air pollution intolerable? Buy an air-filtering unit and stay indoors. Is what comes out of the tap foul to the taste and chock-full of carcinogens? Buy bottled water. And so on. We know it can all happen because it has: I have been doing little more than describing Southern California.

The liberal vision of individuals freely pursuing their own purposes in their own way is a noble one. The mistake comes when it is believed that this is incompatible with collective action and public purpose. Liberal socialism knows that the latter is frequently a condition of the former.

But an ethic of community and mutual responsibility does involve moral choice too. It affirms not merely the fact of community, but also its ethical responsibility. It is quite possible not to believe this. Possessive individualism is a moral choice too; nor is it short of its modern practitioners. We may believe that community is a fiction, that we are not all in it together, that we are not our brother's keeper, that we are not embedded in a social fabric of mutual responsibilities, that we have no obligations beyond the immediately personal and the momentarily chosen. It is not difficult to call in aid a body of doctrine, from the basely vulgar to the elegantly sophisticated, in support of all such negative propositions. But then we have to choose; and socialism has always offered one kind of choice. In this respect it does represent the organization of responsibility.

If socialism has traditionally, and rightly, been associated with a social responsibility for the poor and the vulnerable, this is the reason. The commitment to social inclusion lies at the durable centre of a politics of mutual responsibility. Yet this is properly seen as only one expression of what a responsible society is. It connects with the wider enterprise of 'socializing' responsibility in individuals and organizations. From work to welfare, position to property, parenting to producing, there are obligations as well as freedoms. If liberalism is a doctrine of rights, liberal socialism is a doctrine in which rights are matched by responsibilities. Nor is this merely a banal truism for our troubled times; it provides an active perspective for public policy. It links the reponsibilities of the state to do all it can to provide the opportunities for full citizenship with the responsibilities of individuals, groups, and organizations to respond to those opportunities. That is one kind of mutual responsibility, between the state and its citizens. It is a two-sided deal, not one in which the state merely lectures people on their responsibilities (the New Right version), or one in which people merely demand their rights in relation to the state (the old liberal version). And it requires that the easy rhetoric about the moral responsibilities of the poor and the powerless should be more than matched by a more difficult rhetoric about the social obligations of the rich and powerful. That is what being all in it together means.

THE RESPONSIBLE SOCIETY

What is also clear is that a socialism of community and mutual responsibility is not some kind of soft option, either conceptually or politically. It has none of the comforting props upon which socialism has often rested in the past. It has to live on its own moral, intellectual, and political resources. But it does say some of the most important things that have to be said. A responsible society affirms a relationship between people in society, but also between the state and its citizens. It gives rights, but demands obligations. It offers a stake, but insists that stakeholding carries responsibilities. It also seeks to extend the ways in which responsibility can be actively exercised, through new mechanisms of ownership and control in politics, economy, and society. It provides at least a basis upon which the most challenging responsibility of our time, the care and repair of the natural environment itself, can be engaged with. The shape of a programme, if not the always difficult detail, begins to grow from its philosophical roots.

But no guarantees are attached. Nor do circumstances seem very propitious. One of the many durable insights of R. H. Tawney is that, while people and societies might be free to make choices about how they want to live (leave aside for a moment the question of whether such choice is really chosen), what they are not free to do is to escape the consequences of such choice. A society that repudiated community and responsibility would have to live with the consequences of such irresponsibility. In so far as market individualism does just that, and in so far as that repudiation has been converted into public policy, the consequences that follow are not accidental but inescapable. If the bonds of inclusiveness and security that hold societies together are deliberately fractured, as inequalities grow and divisions widen we should not be surprised if we become a more fractured and fractious society. For some it becomes a drawbridge society, in which private protections are desperately erected against the dangers and de-gradations of the public sphere. For many it presents itself in the crushing contrast between the pavilioned pleasures of the shopping mall and the rampant insecurities outside. The promise of a new freedom begins to feel remarkably like a new kind of servitude. A culture of contentment feels strangely discontented.

The question is whether we – individually, collectively, locally, nation-ally, internationally – have the will, means, and resources to undertake a project of civic renewal. Only a fool would be glibly optimistic, or resignedly pessimistic. There is much that we do not know or understand. In a world of deep uncertainties, an old politics of iron certainties is manifestly out of place. A new politics that is open, pluralistic, and takes political learning seriously is not merely desirable in itself but is a politics for the times. We sense that we are at a moment when quite new ways of living and working, requiring equally new forms of social accounting, may need to be developed in a future that is already pressing in on us. We know that a market economy is the most expedient way of organizing economic life yet devised, and that our prosperity depends upon that economy working vibrantly, but we also know that a market economy without social obligations is a route to hell. We suspect that the way we think about much of this, even the categories we use, may need radical revision before history is much older.

So where, finally, does that leave socialism now? On the one hand, it requires all the modernizing thrust to enable it to learn the lessons of its own past and to develop a repertoire of techniques that has some realistic chance of combining economic dynamism with social decency in the circumstances in which it now finds itself. On the other hand, the demands of revisionism make it even more pressing to be clear about the socialist fundamentals of community and mutual responsiblity. Both are required if socialism is to offer itself as a plausible player in the uncertain years ahead. Such a socialism will be at once manifestly new and conspicuously old. An old collectivism was spawned a century ago as people endeavoured to find a response to the conditions in which they then found themselves. It is at least possible that a new collectivism, of the liberal socialist kind described here, will enable a responsible society to meet the challenges it faces now. But it is the hallmark of this kind of socialism, unlike some of the other kinds discussed earlier, that it rests its fate upon the active choice of free citizens and not upon the destiny of classes or the laws of necessity. A century after his death, it is useful to recall William Morris's description of

> how men fight and lose the battle, and the thing they fought for comes about in spite of their defeat, and when it comes, it turns out not to be what they meant and other men have to fight for what they meant, under another name.

Further reading

The literature of, and on, socialism is vast. The following small selection has therefore been made with two purposes in mind: to enable the reader, first, to fill in some of the history of socialist ideas and movements only touched on briefly and glancingly here, and, second, to read further amongst some of the recent literature on socialism and its late-twentieth-century condition.

Anderson, P., *Considerations on Western Marxism* (London: New Left Books, 1976).

Anderson, P., *In the Tracks of Historical Materialism* (London: Verso, 1983).

Avineri, S., *The Social and Political Thought of Karl Marx* (Cambridge: Cambridge University Press, 1968).

Avineri, S. (ed.), *Varieties of Marxism* (The Hague: Martinus Nijhoff, 1977).

Bahro, R., *The Alternative in Eastern Europe* (London: New Left Books, 1978).

Bahro, R., *Socialism and Survival* (London: Heretic, 1982).

Barry, B., 'The continuing relevance of socialism', in R. Skidelsky (ed.), *Thatcherism* (London: Chatto & Windus, 1988).

Bauman, Z., *Socialism: The Active Utopia* (London: Allen & Unwin, 1976).

Beilharz, P., *Labour's Utopias: Bolshevism, Fabianism and Social Democracy* (London: Routledge, 1991).

Berki, R. N., *Socialism* (London: Dent, 1975).

Bernstein, E., *Evolutionary Socialism* (New York: Schocken, 1961).

Bevan, A., *In Place of Fear* (London: Quartet, 1978).

Blackburn, R. (ed.), *Revolution and Class Struggle: A Reader in Marxist Politics* (London: Fontana, 1977).

Bobbio, N. *Which Socialism?* (Cambridge: Polity, 1988).

Boswell, J., *Community and the Economy* (London: Routledge, 1990).

Bottomore, T., *Sociology and Socialism* (Brighton: Wheatsheaf, 1984).

Brown, B. E. (ed.), *Eurocommunism and Eurosocialism* (New York: Cyrco, 1979).

Brown, G. and Wright, T. (eds) *Values, Visions and Voices: An Anthology of Socialism* (Edinburgh: Mainstream, 1995).

Carrillo, S., *Eurocommunism and the State* (London: Lawrence & Wishart, 1977).

Carver, T., *Marx's Social Theory* (Oxford: Oxford University Press, 1982).

Caute, D., *The Left in Europe Since 1789* (London: Weidenfeld & Nicolson, 1966).

Cohen, S. F., *Bukharin and the Bolshevik Revolution* (Oxford: Oxford University Press, 1980).

Cole, G. D. H., *Self-Government in Industry* (London: Bell, 1917).

Cole, G. D. H., *A History of Socialist Thought* (London: Macmillan, 5 vols, 1953–60).
Crick, B., *In Defence of Politics* (Harmondsworth: Penguin, 2nd edn, 1982).
Crosland, C. A. R., *The Future of Socialism* (London: Cape, 1956).
Crouch, C. and Marquand, D. (eds) *Reinventing Collective Action* (Oxford: Blackwell, 1995).
Denis, N. and Halsey, A. H., *English Ethical Socialism* (Oxford: Clarendon Press, 1988).
Donnison, D., *A Radical Agenda* (London: Rivers Oram, 1991).
Dunn, J., *The Politics of Socialism* (Cambridge: Cambridge University Press, 1984).
Durbin, E., *The Politics of Democratic Socialism* (London: Routledge, 1940).
Elster, J., *Making Sense of Marx* (Cambridge: Cambridge University Press, 1985)
Esping-Anderson, G., *Politics Against Markets: The Social Democratic Road to Power* (Princeton, NJ: Princeton University Press, 1985).
Evans, M., *Karl Marx* (London: Allen & Unwin, 1975).
Femia, J., *Gramsci's Political Thought* (Oxford: Clarendon Press, 1981).
Fried, A. and Sanders, R. (eds), *Socialist Thought: A Documentary History* (Edinburgh: Edinburgh University Press, 1964).
Fukuyama, F., *The End of History and the Last Man* (London: Hamish Hamilton, 1992).
Galbraith, J. K., *The Culture of Contentment* (London: Sinclair-Stevenson, 1992).
Gamble, A., *The Free Economy and the Strong State* (London: Macmillan, 1988).
Gay, P., *The Dilemma of Democratic Socialism: Eduard Bernstein's Challenge to Marx* (New York: Columbia, 1952).
Geras, N., *The Legacy of Rosa Luxemburg* (London: New Left Books, 1976).
Giddens, A., *Beyond Left and Right* (Cambridge: Polity, 1994).
Gorz, A., *Farewell to the Working Class* (London: Pluto, 1982).
Gould, B., *Socialism and Freedom* (London: Macmillan, 1985).
Gould, B., *A Future for Socialism* (London: Cape, 1989).
Gramsci, A., *Selections from the Prison Notebooks*, eds Q. Hoare and G. Nowell Smith (London: Lawrence & Wishart, 1971).
Gray, A., *The Socialist Tradition* (London: Longman, 1946).
Gray. J., *Beyond the New Right* (London: Routledge, 1993).
Gray. J., *The Undoing of Conservatism* (London: Social Market Foundation, 1994).
Gray. J., *After Social Democracy* (London: Demos, 1996).
Hall, S. and Jacques, M. (eds), *New Times* (London: Lawrence & Wishart, 1989).
Harding, N., *Lenin's Political Thought* (London: Macmillan, 1983).
Harrington, M., *Socialism: Past and Present* (New York: Arcade, 1989).
Hattersley, R., *Choose Freedom: The Future for Democratic Socialism* (London: Michael Joseph, 1987).
Held, D., *Models of Democracy* (Cambridge: Polity, 1987).
Hindess, B., *Parliamentary Democracy and Socialist Politics* (London: Routledge & Kegan Paul, 1983).
Hindess, B. (ed.), *Reactions to the Right* (London: Routledge, 1990).
Hirst, P. Q., *Law, Socialism and Democracy* (London: Allen & Unwin, 1986).
Hobsbawm, E. J., *The Forward March of Labour Halted?*, eds M. Jacques and F. Mulhern (London: Verso, 1981).
Hobsbawm, E. J. (ed.), *The History of Marxism: Vol. I, Marxism in Marx's Day* (Brighton: Harvester, 1982).

Hodgson, G., *The Democratic Economy: A New Look at Planning, Markets and Power* (Harmondsworth: Penguin, 1984).
Howe, I. (ed.), *A Handbook of Socialist Thought* (London: Gollancz, 1972).
Hutton, W., *The State We're In* (London: Vintage, 2nd edn, 1996).
Joll, J., *The Second International 1889–1914* (London: Weidenfeld & Nicolson, 1955).
Keane, J., *Democracy and Civil Society* (London: Verso, 1988).
Kitching, G., *Rethinking Socialism* (London: Methuen, 1983).
Knei-Paz, B., *The Social and Political Thought of Leon Trotsky* (Oxford: Oxford University Press, 1978).
Kolakowski, L., *Main Currents of Marxism* (Oxford: OUP, 3 vols., 1978).
Kolakowski, L., and Hampshire, S. (eds), *The Socialist Idea: A Reappraisal* (London: Quartet, 1977).
Le Grand, J. and Estrin, S. (eds), *Market Socialism* (Oxford: Clarendon Press, 1989)
Lichtheim, G., *Marxism* (London: Routledge & Kegan Paul, 1964).
Lichtheim, G., *A Short History of Socialism* (London: Fontana, 1975).
Lindemann, A. S., *A History of European Socialism* (New Haven, CT: Yale, 1983).
Looker, R. (ed.), *Rosa Luxemburg: Selected Political Writings* (London: Cape, 1972).
Luard, E., *Socialism without the State* (London: Macmillan, 1979).
Lukes, S., *Marxism and Morality* (Oxford: Oxford University Press, 1985).
Machin, H. (ed.), *National Communism in Western Europe* (London: Methuen, 1983).
McLellan, D. (ed.), *Karl Marx: Selected Writings* (Oxford: Oxford University Press, 1977).
McLellan, D., *Marxism after Marx* (London: Macmillan, 1979).
McLellan, D. (ed.), *Marx: The First Hundred Years* (London: Fontana, 1983).
Mandel, E., *From Stalinism to Eurocommunism* (London: New Left Books, 1978).
Marquand, D., *The Unprincipled Society* (London: Cape, 1988).
Marquand, D., 'After Socialism', in *Political Studies* xli (1993).
Miliband, D. (ed.), *Reinventing the Left* (Cambridge: Polity, 1994).
Miliband, R., *Marxism and Politics* (Oxford: Oxford University Press, 1977).
Miller, D., *Market, State and Community* (Oxford: Clarendon Press, 1989).
Mills, C. W., *The Marxists* (Harmondsworth: Penguin, 1963).
Nettl, J. P., *Rosa Luxemburg* (Oxford: Oxford University Press, 1969).
Nove, A., *The Economics of Feasible Socialism* (London: Allen & Unwin, 1983).
Offe, C., *Contradictions of the Welfare State*, ed. J. Keane (London: Hutchinson, 1984).
Orwell, G., *The Collected Essays, Journalism and Letters* (London: Secker & Warburg, 4 vols, 1968).
Padgett, S. and Paterson, W. E., *A History of Social Democracy in Postwar Europe* (London: Longman, 1991).
Parekh, B. (ed.), *The Concept of Socialism* (London: Croom Helm, 1975).
Parkin, F., *Marxism and Class Theory: A Bourgeois Critique* (London: Tavistock, 1979).
Paterson, W. E., and Thomas, A. H. (eds.), *The Future of Social Democracy: Problems and Prospects of Social Democratic Parties in Western Europe* (Oxford: Clarendon Press, 1986).
Phillips, A., *Engendering Democracy* (Cambridge: Polity, 1991).
Pierson, C., *Socialism after Communism* (Cambridge: Polity, 1995).

Pimlott, B. (ed.), *Fabian Essays in Socialist Thought* (London: Heinemann, 1984).

Polan, A. J., *Lenin and the End of Politics* (London: Methuen, 1984).

Russell, B., *Roads to Freedom* (London: Allen & Unwin, 1918).

Rustin, M., *For a Pluralist Socialism* (London: Verso, 1985).

Salvadori, M. (ed.), *Modern Socialism* (London: Macmillan, 1968).

Sassoon, D., *One Hundred Years of Socialism* (London: Tauris, 1996).

Scharpf, F., *Crisis and Choice in Swedish Social Democracy* (Ithaca, NY: Cornell University Press, 1991).

Schorske, C. E., *German Social Democracy, 1905–1917* (Cambridge, MA: Harvard, 1955).

Schumpeter, J., *Capitalism, Socialism and Democracy* (London: Allen & Unwin, 1943).

Selbourne, D., *Against Socialist Illusion* (London: Macmillan,1984).

Shaw, G. B. (ed.), *Fabian Essays in Socialism* (London: Allen & Unwin, 6th edn, 1962).

Skidelsky, R., *The World After Communism* (London: Macmillan, 1995).

Tawney, R. H., *Equality* (London: Allen & Unwin, 1964).

Taylor, K., *The Political Ideas of the Utopian Socialists* (London: Cass, 1982).

Thompson, E. P., *The Poverty of Theory and Other Essays* (London: Merlin, 1978).

Tilton, T., *The Political Theory of Swedish Social Democracy* (Oxford: Clarendon Press, 1991).

Tudor, H. and Tudor, J. M. (eds), *Marxism and Social Democracy: The Revisionist Debate 1896–1898* (Cambridge: Cambridge University Press, 1988).

Wainwright, H., *Arguments for a New Left* (Oxford: Blackwell, 1994).

Waller, M., Coppieters, B. and Deschouwer, K. (eds), *Social Democracy in a Post-Communist Europe* (London: Cass, 1994).

Walzer, M., *Spheres of Justice* (New York: Basic Books, 1983).

Williams, R., *Keywords* (London: Croom Helm, 1976).

Williams, R., *Towards 2000* (London: Chatto & Windus, 1983).

Williams, R., *Resources of Hope* (London: Verso, 1989).

Wilson, E., *To the Finland Station* (London: Fontana, 1960).

Woodcock, G., *Anarchism* (Harmondsworth: Penguin, 1963).

Worsley, P., *Marx and Marxism* (London: Tavistock, 1982).

Wright, A. W., *G. D. H. Cole and Socialist Democracy* (Oxford: Clarendon Press, 1979).

Wright, A. W. (ed.), *British Socialism: Socialist Thought from the 1880's to the 1960's* (London: Longman, 1983).

Wright, A. W., *R. H. Tawney* (Manchester: Manchester University Press, 1987).

Index

actors/agency 87–104; agents of
socialism 87–91; class and party
91–7; class and people 101–4; new
actors and new problems 97–101
anarchism 6
arguments 18–34; and ambiguities
25–7; common and uncommon
ground 21–5; definitions 18–21;
forms of socialist argument 32–4;
science and history 28–30; values
and plurality 31–4
associational socialism 80
Attlee, C. 67
authoritarianism 77–80, 106
autogestion 85

Bad Godesberg programme 15, 85, 102
Bakunin, M. 5, 74
Bauer, O. 15
Benn, T. 128–9
Bernstein, E. 10, 43, 45–6, 57–8
Bevan, A. 68, 123
Blair, T. 135
Blanc, L. 5, 53
Blanquism 5, 53, 55
Blum, L. 137
Bolsheviks 3; renaming as Communist
Party 12; revolution
11–12, 44, 70–1, 98, 99
Bottomore, T. 19, 118
'boundary problem' 103
bourgeois consciousness 94–5
bourgeoisie 89
Britain 14, 72, 117; actors 102;
collectivism 10, 80–3, 134–5;
constitutionalism 10, 61, 62;

doctrines 35–6, 46; Labour Party
see Labour Party; Liberal Party
129, 130; recent socialist thinking
124–36; Social Democratic Party
4, 109, 129, 130; socialist traditions
9–10
bureaucracy, state 73–4, 77–80

capitalism 5, 104; arguments 21–4;
distribution and social justice
118–19; ideological hegemony
111–12; Marxism and collapse of
43; post-communist countries and
137–8; social democracy and
welfare 108–10
capitalist democracy 111–14, 119–20
certainty 43–6
Charter 88, 133
China 98
choice 141; responsible society 147–8
citizenship 132
class 27; agency 87–104 *passim*; Marx
5, 28–9, 48, 54; and party
87–8, 91–7, 97–8; and people 101–4;
see also bourgeoisie, working class
Clause IV 126, 135
Cole, G. D. H. 70, 81, 82
collectivism 126; Britain
10, 80–3, 134–5; gradualist 10;
liberal socialism 140–1, 145;
structures 80–3
communism 2–3, 15–16, 83, 117;
appropriation of Marxism 111; end
of and capitalism 137–8;
Eurocommunism
15, 64–5, 85, 103, 107–8; methods

53, 61, 63–4; party dictatorship 70, 82; reformism 85–6; rupture with socialism 12; and social democracy 106–8
Communist (Third) International 12, 15, 61, 80
Communist Party of the Soviet Union 12
community ethic 136–7, 141–2; relevance of socialism 144–7
consciousness 93–5
Conservative Party, British 125; *see also* New Right, Thatcher Government
constitutional reform 133
constitutionalism 10, 61–2, 65, 68
'council' movement 79
credible socialism 114–17
Crosland, A. 108, 126–7

decentralization 133
definitions of socialism 18–21
democracy 74; capitalist 111–14, 119–20; defining socialism 19–20; liberal socialism 141; participatory 77–80, 84, 85, 128; social democracy and 107; and socialism 65–8
democratic socialism 3–4, 82–3; Britain 46; critique of Marxism 49–50; enabling socialism 84–6; methods 66–8; third way 121–3; *see also* social democracy
dependency 109
despotism 73–4, 77–80
determinism 47–9
distribution 109–10, 118–19
diversity 13–17
doctrines 35–51; British Labour Party 126–7; class, party and ideology 94–5; dangers of doctrine 46–51; kinds of doctrine 35–40; Marxism 40–3, 110–13; socialism and certainty 43–6
Dunn, J. 74, 114–15, 116

Eastern and Central Europe 138
economic development 105–6
economism 48
enabling socialism 84–6

enabling state 132
ends, means and 68
Engels, F. 1, 6; *Anti-Dühring* 8, 41; constitutional politics 58–9; 'scientific' socialism 7–8; socialism and communism 2–3; systematization of Marxism 41
environment 119
equality 31–2, 71; social democracy 108–10
ethical socialism 9–10, 46, 80; *see also* moralism, values
Eurocommunism 15, 64–5, 85, 103, 107–8
European Community 133
example 122
experience, strategy and 62–5

Fabianism/Fabian Society 10, 46, 62, 102, 105–6, 134; state 80–1
fascism 47, 88
fellow-travelling 47
feminism 104
First International 7
Fourier, F.M.C. 4, 88
France 7, 85
freedom *see* liberty
Fukuyama, F. 142
futures 105–23; credible socialism 114–17; mirage of Marxism 111–14; 1900 and present day 105–8; present state of socialism 118–21; social democracy's dilemmas 108–10; third way 121–3

Gaitskell, H. 127
Galbraith, J.K. 138
general strike 61–2
Germany 47, 85; Social Democratic Party *see* Social Democratic Party
global humanism 121
Gorz, A. 71, 90
government 115–16
gradualist collectivism 10
Gramsci, A. 79
guild socialism 81

Hansson, P. A. 102
Hardie, K. 10, 80
Hattersley, R. 130

history 42–3, 89; science and 28–30
Hobsbawm, E. 103, 131–2
Holland, S. 128
human nature 32, 115
Hutton, W. 140

imperialism, western 98–9
Independent Labour Party (Britain) 10
individual, state and 145–6
individualism: contrasted with
    socialism 21–2, 23; market 86, 141–4
Institute of Public Policy Research 134
insurrectionism 5, 53, 55
international socialism
    10–11, 12–13, 42–3, 59–61; *see also*
    First International, Second
    International, Third International
International Working Men's
    Association (First International) 7

Jaurès, J. 7, 46, 83, 101

Kautsky, K. 8, 46, 48, 63, 78; class
    93–4, 94–5; doctrinal orthodoxy
    42–3; revolution 57, 60; structure 72
Kinnock, N. 129–30
Kitching, G. 20
knowledge 116–17

labour movement 54, 63, 92, 131;
    British and state 72; need to become
    more than a labour movement 121
Labour Party, British
    82, 102, 117, 123, 124–36; Clause IV
    126, 135; election defeats 125, 127,
    128, 129–30, 135; living off the past
    125–7; *Meet the Challenge, Make
    the Change* 133; new revisionism
    131–6; 1945 government 2; policy
    review 130–1, 132–5; problems in
    the 1980s 127–31; revisionism
    126–7
Labour Representation Committee 126
labourism 126
Lassalle, F. 5, 53
Lenin, V.I.: Bolshevism 11–12; class
    and party 92–6, 97–8, 100;
    doctrinaire socialism 45; and the end
    of politics 76–80; and Luxemburg
    59–60; morality 50; revolution

60–1, 63–4; rupture within
    socialism 11
Leninism 12, 45, 63; methods and
    revisionism 56–62; Marxism-
    Leninism 12, 45–6, 61
liberal democracy 65–8
Liberal Party, British 129, 130
liberal socialism 139–41, 143–4
liberalism 24–5
liberation movement 121
libertarian socialism 25, 85
liberty 31; political 107, 120; state and
    73–4, 145
Lowenthal, R. 19
Luxemburg, R. 43, 63, 78–9, 96–7; and
    revisionism 59–60

Mann, T. 80
market 118–19; social 129; state and
    121–2, 139–41, 142–3, 143–4, 145–6
market individualism 86, 141–4
market socialism 133
Marquand, D. 138
Marx, K.: antipathy towards socialism
    2–3, 4; doctrines 36, 38–40; and
    modernization 24; political economy
    48–9; production theory of society
    28–9, 38, 72–3; proletarian revolution
    30, 89–91, 92–3; revolution and
    reform 53–6; 'scientific' socialism
    7–8, 38; self-emancipation of
    proletariat 96–7; structural vacuum
    72–6; and 'utopian' socialism
    1–2, 4–5, 37, 72, 88–9
Marxism 4, 21, 83, 110, 117; agency 91;
    ascendancy 5–6, 40; dangers of
    doctrine 49–51; doctrines
    40–3, 110–13; failure of proletarian
    revolution 99–101; as ideology 8–9;
    Professorial 110, 112; prospects for
    socialism 105–6, 111–14; Russia
    11–12, 63; Second International
    period 6–8, 8–9, 54; and social
    democracy 63–5
Marxism-Leninism 12, 45–6, 61
methods/means 52–68; democracy and
    socialism 65–8; reform and
    revolution 52–6; revisionism and
    Leninism 56–62; strategy and
    experience 62–5

modernization 22–4
modesty 116–17
moralism 35–40, 50, 51, 121; *see also*
   ethical socialism, values
Morris, W. 9, 44, 80, 149
mutual responsibility 136–7, 144–7;
   responsible society 147–9

national communism 98–9
nationalism 42
nationalization 82–3
Nazi Party 88
neo-liberal conservatism *see* New Right
new revisionism 131–6
New Right 70, 109, 117, 125, 142–3
non-collectivist tradition 5
Nove, A. 19, 73

oppression 98
organizational socialism 25–6, 80–1;
   state 71–2
Orwell, G. 84, 115
Owen, R. 4
ownership 121–2; private 118–19;
   public 20, 82–3, 128

Paris Commune 75, 77
parliamentarism 10, 61–2, 65, 68
Parti Ouvrier Français 7
participatory democracy
   77–80, 84, 85, 128
party: activists 128; class and 87–8,
   91–7, 97–8
party-states 15–16, 77–80, 106, 111
peasantry 98–9
people: as socialist actors 101–4; *see*
   also human nature
Petrović, G. 19
planning 71; British Labour Party
   128, 133; credible socialism
   115–16, 121–2; enabling socialism
   85–6
Plekhanov, G.V. 43
pluralism 85–6; values and 31–4
policy review 130–1, 132–5
political action 47, 68
political freedom 107, 120
politics: Lenin and the end of 76–80;
   Marxian vacuum 55–6, 72–6, 113
possibilists 6

Poulantzas, N. 103
power 121–2, 141
private ownership 118–19
producer militancy 61–2
production: Marx's theory of
   28–9, 38, 72–3; social democracy's
   dilemmas 109–10
Professorial Marxism 110, 112
proletarian dictatorship 75–6
proletarianization 90–1
proletariat *see* working class/proletariat
property *see* ownership
Proudhon, P.J. 1–2, 4, 53
public ownership 20, 82–3, 128
public purpose 144–5
public services 140

radicalization 110
rationalism 26–7, 28–30; doctrines and
   moralism 35–40
reductionism 48
reformism: betrayal of working class
   100–1; Eurocommunism 108;
   expectations 105–6; and revolution
   52–65; traditions 6, 10
relevance of socialism 144–7
repressive state bureaucracy
   73–4, 77–80
resolute constitutionalism 10
resource allocation 115–16
responsibility, mutual 136–7, 144–7
responsible society 147–9
revisionism 45–6; British Labour Party
   126–7 (new revisionism 131–6);
   reform and revolution 52, 56–62; *see*
   also Bernstein
revolution 105–6; actors 88–98
   passim; reform and 52–65
   (controversy in SPD 56–61)
Right, New 70, 109, 117, 125, 142–3
Russia/Soviet Union 11–12, 106;
   Bolshevik revolution
   11–12, 44, 70–1, 98, 99; dangers of
   doctrine 47; repressive communism
   15–16; socialist centre of gravity
   13–14; transition to communism 12

Saint-Simon, C. H. 4, 26, 37, 88
Schumpeter, J. 19
'scientific' socialism 7–8, 57; doctrines

37–45 *passim*; and history 28–30; and market individualism 142; state despotism 74

Second International 57, 59, 99, 101, 126; collapse 10–11; German SPD 6–7, 54; Marxism 6–8, 8–9, 54; revisionism and Leninism 59–61

Section Français de l'Internationale Ouvrière (SFIO) 7

self-administration 77–80, 84, 85

Shaw, G. B. 19, 62, 80, 114

Skidelsky, R. 142

Smith, J. 135

social change 48

social democracy: actors 93–4; betrayal of working class 100–1, 111; British Labour Party 136; collectivism 80–3; communism and 106–8; dilemmas 108–10; Eurocommunism 64; methods 56–62, 65–8; structures 70–1; substitution of people for class 102–3; tradition 3–4, 15, 46; *see also* democratic socialism

Social Democratic Party, British 4, 109, 129, 130

Social Democratic Party, German (SPD) 47; Bad Godesberg programme 15, 85, 102; revolution vs reform 56–61; Second International 6–7, 54

social market 129

Socialist International *see* international socialism, First International, Second International, Third International

Socialist Philosophy Group 134

socialist regimes 15–16, 77–80, 106, 111

Sorel, G. 44, 61–2, 91–2

Soviet Union *see* Russia/Soviet Union

Spain 115

Spartacus League 96

state: credible socialism 115–16, 121–2; democratic socialism 82–3, 86; enabling 132; liberal socialism 139–41, 142–3, 143–4; and liberty 73–4, 145; market and 121–2, 139–41, 142–3, 143–4, 145–6; Marx 55–6; Marxism 113;

organizational socialism 71–2; social democracy 109–10

state action tradition 5

state despotism 73–4, 77–80

statism 69–72

Strachey, J. 44

strategy 62–5

structures 69–86; collectivism 80–3; enabling socialism 84–6; Lenin and end of politics 76–80; Marxian vacuum 72–6; socialism and statism 69–72

substitutism 87–8

supply-side socialism 133

Sweden 85, 102, 106

syndicalism 8–9, 61–2, 81, 91–2

Tawney, R. H. 66–7, 102, 147–8

Taylor, C. 19

technological change 119

Thatcher Government 125, 129

Thatcherism 125; *see also* New Right

theory *see* doctrines

Third (Communist) International 12, 15, 61, 80

Third World socialisms 15–16

trade-unionism 95; *see also* labour movement

traditions 1–17; disintegration and diversity 13–17; and divisions 9–13; Marxism as ideology 8–9; words and 1–8

Turin workers' council movement 79

'Two-and-a-Half International' 13

'utopian' socialism 29, 40, 53; Marx and 1–2, 4–5, 37, 72, 88–9

values 20–1, 121, 139; and plurality 31–4; *see also* ethical socialism, moralism

Webb, B. 8–9, 82

Webb, S. 22, 23, 82

welfare 32, 107, 132–3; social democracy's dilemmas 108–10

Wells, H. G. 26–7

western imperialism 98–9

Williams, R. 84

Wilson, H. 127

workers' democracy 77–80, 84, 85, 128
working class/proletariat 39; agency
 88–104 *passim*; general strike 61–2;

Luxemburg 60; proletarian
 dictatorship 75–6
World War I 10–11